Objectivity in social science

Objectivity in social science

FRANK CUNNINGHAM

University of Toronto Press

© University of Toronto Press 1973
Toronto and Buffalo
Printed in Canada
ISBN 0-8020-1943-9
Microfiche ISBN 0-8020-0287-0
LC 72-95461

CONTENTS

PREFACE

My interest in the subject of objectivity in the social sciences derives from two sources, one pedagogic and one political. With many other teachers I have long been frustrated by a wall of agnosticism which so often thwarts attempts to initiate class debate about the relative merits of rival positions in political philosophy or social theory. The attitude that such debate is futile, since nobody can ever know which position is objectively superior, is, I believe, one of the most widespread among North American high school and college social science students, and many of their teachers as well (rivalled only by the belief that men are inherently aggressive and selfish).

No doubt some espouse anti-objectivism simply because it is part of the conventional wisdom, and some because it provides an excuse, so to speak, for avoiding the very hard work of evaluating general theories. But there are two additional sources of anti-objectivism. One is the all too frequently encountered phenomenon of the hypocritical 'objectivist,' the social theorist who couches his work in the language of rigorous scientific objectivity and who prefaces his views with pious statements about the need for objectivity, but whose conclusions are easily seen to be nothing but rationalizations for some social view he antecedently holds or believes it opportune to hold, not at all supported by the objective methods he advocates using. It is not surprising that many students become cynical about the objective reliability of any social-scientific studies as they encounter more and more of these hypocritical works.

Of course failure to find truly objective studies does not prove the *impossibility* of such studies, and it is here that the other source of anti-objectivist attitudes becomes important. The situation which is of primary concern in this book is that students of social science are confronted with a host of arguments favouring anti-objectivism, often in popular texts, usually eloquently written, advanced along with insightful comments on the history of science, the inobvious effects of bias, and so on, and often drawn from popularized theories in the philosophies of science, language, and perception. These arguments confront one with an overwhelming maze, and have convinced many either that objectivity in social science is impossible or that the question of whether it is possible or not is itself too complicated for any but the experts, and the experts are divided.

On the political side it has been largely by a study of human history and society that I have come to adopt the theory and practice of scientific socialism, or Marxism. This has given rise to concern with the question of objectivity on two scores. Given the importance to one's life activity of adopting this position, it is at least unsettling to come across arguments which, if correct, would show that I am deluded in thinking I have been led to my views objectively and that I might as well have adopted any other position, or even none at all. Then again, in attempting to defend and to develop Marxism I have encountered a strange state of affairs. On the one hand, I have found Marxism challenged by its opponents more and more *not* because they think it is empirically false, but because, according to some of these opponents, Marxists claim that their findings are objectively true (not realizing, it is said, the vanity or even 'totalitarianism' of belief in objectivity), or because, according to other opponents, Marxism suffers from the internal contradiction that, if its explanations of the origins of social-scientific views were correct, then it would follow that no social-scientific explanations (including those of the Marxist himself) could be objective. On the other hand, I have found some who claim to be *adherents* of Marxism arguing that its findings necessitate that the claim to objectivity is at best a practice-inhibiting delusion and at worst counter-revolutionary.

Both these opponents and adherents of Marxism share the view that objectivity in social science is impossible, and in probing for their defences of the view I have found that, stripped of rhetoric, the arguments which they employ are the very same as those which have proven convincing to so many students of social theory. Moreover examination of these arguments has convinced me that the position of anti-objectivism is false and that belief in anti-objectivism on the part of Marxists is a hindrance to the scientific development and application of Marxism (in which Marxism's merits relative to rival theories are best determined).

This work, then, and my PH D thesis of the same title on which it is based (University of Toronto, January 1970), were written to combat the position of anti-objectivism by drawing together and criticizing the recurrent arguments in its favour.

While statements of anti-objectivist arguments have been taken from authors most often appealed to in defense of anti-objectivism, like P.K. Feyerabend, Thomas Kuhn, and Benjamin Lee Whorf, the book is a survey of representative arguments, not of the development and details of the theories of individual authors. Similarly, while some epistemological points are made, the bulk of the book treats anti-objectivist arguments short of dealing with very basic epistemological issues (e.g., about epistemological scepticism or general theories of truth). My justification for this is that it is not necessary to delve exhaustively into the deeper regions of epistemology to show the inadequacies of anti-objectivist arguments insofar as they are a source of concern to students of society, and in any case defending objectivism at that level requires separate works, some of which already exist and are referred to where appropriate. What I have attempted to offer is, at the least, a convenient map for finding one's way about in the tangle of issues surrounding the question of objectivity in social science, and, at the most, a set of arguments sufficient to convince the perplexed and the presently wrong-headed of the (objective) falsity of social-scientific anti-objectivism.

I should like to extend special thanks for their assistance in reading and criticizing the manuscript at one or more stages in its career to D.P. Gauthier (who directed the thesis), D. Goldstick, B. Mossop, J.M.O. Wheatley, and F.F. Wilson, and to R. Fairey for typing the manuscript and University of Toronto Press for assistance in editing. The book has been published with the help of a grant from the Humanities Research Council of Canada, using funds provided by the Canada Council.

F.C. *Toronto July 1972*

Objectivity in social science

CHAPTER ONE Objectivism and anti-objectivism

Criticisms of the possibility of objectivity in the social sciences are as old as the social sciences themselves. The Cambridge Platonists and others argued the issue against Hobbes, and the German idealist philosophers argued it against contemporary rationalists and material-ists. Most of the arguments offered by these philosophers against the possibility of objectivity miss the mark, often being not criticisms of the possibility of objectivity at all, but rather moral condemnations of carry-ing on any social science, objectively or otherwise. However in recent years the debate has taken on new life, sparked by contemporary work in the philosophies of science, language, and perception, which has given anti-objectivists a core of fresh arguments with which to support their position.

The central task of this work will be to examine critically this core of arguments. While this examination cannot claim to be exhaustive, I believe that at the least it can provide a guide through current, popular arguments for anti-objectivism in the social sciences to show that they are inadequate as they stand, and that, short of embracing a thorough-going scepticism which would make all knowledge impossible, support for these arguments from other quarters is not as promising as many social theorists and philosophers of social science seem to think.

The word 'objective' is often used loosely to mean 'disinterested,' or simply 'true.' But, if unqualified, neither of these captures the meaning of 'objective.' A scientist may well have a strong personal stake in arriv-ing at some conclusion, but be objective in his inquiries all the same; and a person might arrive at true conclusions by non-objective means (or false conclusions by objective ones). The term is also used by philosophers of a phenomenological bent, like Stephen Strasser, and by social theorists like Ludwig von Mises and F.A. Hayek, to mean 'having to do with objects' (i.e., non-human things) as opposed to 'subjects' (human agents).[1] This use is obviously only verbally similar to the one in question. It derives from a view sometimes called 'subjectivism' (most famously argued for by Max Weber), which has to do with the scope of social science. The subjectivist argues that social-scientific inquiry ought to be restricted to 'meaningful' (generally conscious) behaviour,[2] but while it will be seen that subjectivism may be appealed to for one kind of argument against objectivism, the two views are not necessarily opposed.[3] (For this reason an opponent of objectivism will be called an anti-objectivist rather than a subjectivist.)

Beyond these verbal difficulties the characterization of objectivism can be made into a philosophical problem in itself by introducing recent debates about the 'correspondence theory of truth.' For the most part this debate will not be entered into. In the present work I am addressing those students and would-be students of human society who agree that, if a reliable science of society is possible, it will be one that reaches conclusions which are true to the extent that the properties attributed to a society in the conclusions are properties which that society does have.[4]

An adequate characterization of objectivism, then, seems to me this: that it is possible for an inquiry to be objective if, and only if, a / it is possible for its descriptions and explanations of a subject-matter to reveal the actual nature of that subject-matter, where 'actual nature' means 'the qualities and relations of a subject-matter as they exist independently of an inquirer's thoughts and desires regarding them,' and b / it is not possible for two inquirers holding rival theories about some subject-matter and having complete knowledge of each other's theories (including the grounds for holding them) both to be justified[5] in adhering to their theories. The second condition is necessary to exclude from being considered as objectivists those relativists who deny that it can be justified to adopt and sustain belief in one theory to the exclusion of others on non-pragmatic grounds. (There are theorists who deny that a social science can meet one or both of these conditions, but who wish to retain the word 'objective' in other senses as applicable to scientific inquiry. Relevant views of some of these theorists are discussed in chapter 5 under the heading 'the new objectivities,' but in the main I am not concerned with the terminological propriety of such work usage, and will consider the theorists in question opponents of 'objectivism' as the term is used in this work, whose substantive views must be countered, expressly or by implication.)

Other uses of 'objective' in this work are derivative from this one. For example, to say that the conclusions of a social-scientific theory are objectively true is to say (redundantly) that the qualities and relations

attributed by its conclusions to a subject-matter are those actually possessed by that subject-matter, and to say that an inquirer is objective in
his choices from among rival theories is to say that he pursues his inquiry
in a way that enables him (not necessarily always or infallibly) to arrive
at objectively true conclusions. Thus put, the thesis being argued here
is that it is possible for there to be objective choices in social science.

As this characterization suggests, the focus of the present examination
will be on the possibility of objectivity, but considerations of actual
social-scientific practice (and the practice of other sciences) will be seen
to be relevant.

In order to uncover the core of arguments on which anti-objectivist
claims rest it will be useful first to list some theses which are not necessarily involved in objectivism (contrary to what would-be defenders of
anti-objectivism sometimes think), and then briefly to indicate the failings of some popular, though as they stand almost obviously inadequate,
defences of anti-objectivism. Objectivism neither is nor need include the
following positions.

Objectivism is not *positivism*. Some assume that the only alternative
to anti-objectivism is what they call positivism;[6] however on any
interpretation of positivism it can be seen that this is not the case. An
objectivist need not adopt the verification theory of meaning (although
he must adopt the entirely different view that scientific conclusions are
objectively verifiable). Nor is he committed to the denial of there being
synthetic *a priori* truths (although whether or not he denies this, he will
have to hold that there are at least some synthetic *a posteriori* truths,
on pain of too severely limiting the range of objectively determinable
facts in social science, and he will have to deny Kant's account of the
possibility of synthetic *a priori* truths, which, as will be seen, supports
anti-objectivism).

Finally, and this is what anti-objectivists who charge objectivists with
positivism seem most often to mean by the charge, objectivism does not
require that there be some basic, irreducible elements which can serve
as final courts of appeal in evaluating theories. Suppose a theory T is
proposed as an explanation of some subject-matter and that this subject-
matter is analyzed into components A, B, and C related in certain ways
by T; further suppose that each component is again analyzable (by T or
some other theory) into other components (A into a, b, and c, etc.), and
so on indefinitely or infinitely. What effect could this have on the objectivity of T? Surely the mere fact of indefinite analyzability can have no
effect on the objectivity argument, which in this case will only be that

there is some way of determining objectively whether the subject-matter in question *is* A, B, and C (also whether A *is* a, b, and c, etc.).[7]

Objectivism in social science is not *behaviourism*.[8] Unless a very strict version of behaviourism is correct (a state of affairs which the anti-objectivist who identifies behaviourism with objectivism could not welcome), an objectivist can argue that statements about intervening, mental variables can be objectively arrived at and sustained.

Nor is the objectivist committed to *determinism*.[9] In the case, for example, of microphysics, a scientist may hold to indeterminism and also maintain that probability laws can be objectively determined. And in social science one may, as in the case of Talcott Parsons at one point in his career, be a libertarian; and while that may limit his social science to taxonomies of character types (since causal laws would be hard to maintain), within those limits he may consistently hold to objectivism. Thus he can hold that the applications of the taxonomies are objectively determinable, i.e., that is possible to describe objectively social phenomena using the language of the taxonomies. Closely related to this is that objectivism does not entail predictability. Theorists who hold that prediction is not possible in social science (because of the uniqueness or historical nature of its subject-matter or the possibility of 'suicidal' and 'self-fulfilling' predictions) sometimes speak as if they were defending anti-objectivism thereby. But again, while the kinds of conclusions which can be objectively established will be severely limited by the soundness of these arguments, the objectivist position itself will not be refuted.

Objectivism is not *inductivism*.[10] As will be argued, objectivists are committed to the non-theory-ladenness (in one sense) of descriptions and laws, but are not committed to the abandonment of theory altogether or to any doctrine prescribing the temporal priority of inductive work to theorizing in scientific inquiry (inductivism in its strong and its weak senses). In the first place, objectivists claim objectivity for *theoretical* laws as well as for observation laws, and in the second place, it is possible for an objectivist to hold that theories may be necessary to guide one in scientific inquiry as long as he still maintains that the fruits of that inquiry can be objectively held.

Similarly objectivity is not *detachment* from the extra-scientific demands of social, political, and personal life.[11] The question which confronts the objectivist is not whether scientists do (or should) have any extra-scientific interests in the outcome of their work – few could deny this – but whether it is possible, regardless of other interests, for a scientist to carry on that work objectively. If a psychological argument were offered to the effect that *any* extra-scientific interests are certain to prevent a scientist from attaining objectivity, then the objectivist would be committed to holding that scientists must be detached. But the promise of such an argument seems slim.

Advocates of positions falsely equated with either objectivism or anti-objectivism often debate their views in ways that bear on the gaining of objectively true conclusions in the social sciences. For instance, critics of subjectivism maintain that, by disallowing explanation by reference to extra-subjective factors in all phases of inquiry, the subjectivist is likely to present a fragmentary and distorted picture of the very subjective states and processes that interest him, and advocates of free will charge that deterministic accounts fail to capture what is most important about human nature. But in such debates the question of objectivism versus anti-objectivism does not arise. Rather, advocates of opposing sides of the debates generally assume that objectivity is possible and debate about how (objectively) true conclusions are most likely to be reached. In this respect arguments which hinge on equating objectivism or anti-objectivism with one of the positions discussed above differ from three arguments which *do* directly challenge objectivism. These arguments, especially widespread among social theorists, are what might be called the argument from values, historicism, and the argument from selection. Despite their popularity, however, these arguments cannot by themselves support anti-objectivism, and it is best to get clear of them from the outset.

THE ARGUMENT FROM VALUES

Arguments from values start from the undeniable fact that scientists, social and otherwise, are not robots, but humans with human values, and their values often play a role in their selection of problems and in the conclusions they reach. Most of these arguments do not have to do with scientific objectivity, or indeed with the content of scientific inquiry at all, but only with the uses to which such inquiry is put. Thus, for example, Max Weber's classic statement of the so-called value problem:

The *significance* of a configuration of cultural phenomena and the basis of this significance cannot however be derived and rendered intelligible by a system of analytical laws ... however perfect it may be, since the significance of cultural events pre-supposes a *value-orientation* towards these events.[12]

The context of Weber's argument makes it clear that 'significance' means 'importance' here; hence the argument has to do only with the selection of a subject-matter to be studied and not with the conclusions which can be reached. It does not bear on the question of objectivity.[13]

Gunnar Myrdal has devoted much of his efforts toward showing the place of values within the social sciences, that is, the influence of the social scientist's values on his drawing of conclusions. But despite Myrdal's occasional comments endorsing anti-objectivism (and those of anti-objectivists who praise his work too hastily), the arguments he gives do not militate against objectivism. For instance, Myrdal begins his *Value in Social Theory* by suggesting that the conclusions of a social-scientific study are necessarily determined by the social scientist's values, but as his argument develops it turns out that a scientist's values provide rather 'a definition of relevant interests,' and Myrdal's position becomes similar to that of Weber on this point.[14] In his more recent *Objectivity in Social Research* Myrdal (again despite some undefended comments to the contrary) is primarily concerned to show that no social scientist can be disinterested (in the sense of having no value attitudes toward his subject-matter) and that, even while proclaiming their complete objectivity, social scientists are often unwittingly biased. His conclusion is that values should be made explicit so as to avoid bias.[15]

It cannot be denied that scientists are sometimes biased in drawing conclusions The propensities, especially in the social sciences, to jump to hasty conclusions (or to refuse unjustifiably to draw a conclusion), to ignore some data while distorting others, etc., are well known. But these facts do not show that objectivity is impossible, just that objectively pursued inquiry is difficult. So two kinds of arguments have been advanced in support of the general argument from values. One is raised in a typical way by James Leach:

... two inquirers, with the same evidence and making the same probability assignments, might nonetheless rationally disagree about the acceptability of a given explanatory hypothesis on the basis of attaching different values to the seriousness in action of making a mistake. The case against [value neutrality] seems best argued, then, on the grounds of recent work in statistical analysis concerned with the problem of rational decision making in the face of uncertainty.[16]

Insofar as Leach's argument is limited to probability laws and hypotheses, it does not disprove the possibility of objectivity, since it is at least possible, by discovering some theory which explains why certain laws hold only approximately and which can supplement those laws with other, non-probabilistic ones, to remove the uncertainty of probabilistic explanations in any one case.[17] However as the argument is developed to the effect that there will always be insufficient data to justify objectively deciding for accepting a hypothesis (or deciding for one over another), whether the hypothesis is probabilistic or not, due to the fact that no hypothesis is ever absolutely confirmed, Leach's position seems to be more strongly anti-objectivist.

This kind of argument will be further discussed below in connection with the argument from selection, but suffice it to note here that, as it stands, the argument is surely too strong. It may well be that increasing observation and experimentation will increasingly tend to confirm (and therefore possibly disconfirm) a hypothesis and that there is no upper limit to such confirmation; thus there will never be sufficient data to confirm a hypothesis absolutely; and therefore estimates of the importance of acting on a hypothesis will be involved in deciding on cut-off points. But objectivity need not require the absolute confirmability of hypotheses. To show that objectivity is possible it is enough to indicate that, in any circumstance in which a scientist decides that observations are sufficient to justify him (given his ends, etc.) in cutting off observation and calling a hypothesis empirically confirmed, it is always possible that further observation will lead him (or others) *objectively* to alter this decision. Perhaps the appeal of this argument depends on confusing the objectivity of scientific decisions and the objectivity of scientific conclusions. A scientist's conclusions may at some time be shown to be objectively wrong, even though, given his aims, values, and the knowledge available to him, his decision might have been objective.

The second kind of support for the argument from value involves what Nagel has called 'characterizing' value judgments. This is the view that to do justice to his subject-matter a social scientist must be able to distinguish those characteristics of his subject-matter which are essentially value characteristics (ones of which valuation is appropriate or even morally obligatory). Thus Nagel quotes Leo Strauss:

The prohibition against value-judgments in social science [purportedly so as to preserve objectivity] would lead to the consequence that we are permitted to give a strictly factual description of the overt acts that can be observed in concentration camps, and perhaps an equally factual analysis of the motivations of the actors concerned: we would not be permitted to speak of cruelty.[18]

Of course a social scientist can describe a person or act as cruel, and in so doing he may also be expressing moral disapproval of that act or person, but this does not mean that the description 'cruel' cannot be objectively ascribed. Nagel argues that a social scientist's value judgments (or as Nagel calls them 'appraising' judgments) are not necessary conditions for such characterizations.[19] What is more, there is a sense in which the reverse of the anti-objectivist's argument is true, that objective characterization is necessary for evaluation. Presumably the social scientist could list characteristics which in his view attach to a person or act which he considers himself justified in calling cruel, and then it would be open for him to determine objectively whether or not the act or person in question did or did not have those characteristics.

It may be logically impossible sincerely to describe something in moral language (e.g., as 'morally bad'), without taking a moral stance (e.g., of censure) toward that thing, but it requires additional argument to show that having this attitude is a prerequisite for recognizing or characterizing the thing. Two views, usually advanced by philosophers of history, are sometimes thought to provide the basis for such an argument, though it does not seem to me that they help the anti-objectivist here. One view is that advanced by R.G. Collingwood, who distinguishes between the 'inside' and the 'outside' of an action, the latter being the external, observable movements of someone, the former his motives or purposes in acting as he does.[20] It is on the basis of this kind of view that Isaiah Berlin, among others, criticizes those who urge historians:

... to suppress even that minimal degree of moral or psychological evaluation which is necessarily involved in viewing human beings as creatures with purposes and motives (and not merely as causal factors in the procession of events) ...[21]

The point is that in describing someone's action (in Collingwood's sense of 'action') it makes a difference whether we call what he did a murder or a killing, for example, and which of these we call it will depend upon what we think his motives were and how we evaluate acts done out of such motives.

A second possible basis of the anti-objectivist argument under consideration has to do with one view of historical explanation. William Dray argues that to explain an action is to show that doing it was appropriate to the circumstances in which it was performed, and determining what is appropriate involves 'an element of appraisal of what was done.'[22] So it might be argued that this appraisal may involve value judgments, just as Dray argues that, given the concept of 'cause,' historians employ value judgments in assigning causes to historical events.[23]

But neither of these views seems to me to offer the anti-objectivist independent support. Surely it is possible to state objectively the characteristics of someone's purposes which lead some to call his action murder, even though one does not consider the purposes murderous. Two people might agree on the characteristics of a purposeful action, yet disagree on whether the action is morally blameworthy, as in the case of those who differ on whether legal executions are murders. And likewise it seems that those characteristics of an action which lead an inquirer to judge the action appropriate to certain circumstances can also be objectively described both by him and by someone who does not agree (on normative or non-normative grounds) that such an action is appropriate to the circumstances.

Some of the reasons why anti-objectivist arguments from value might have special appeal are worth noting here. One has to do with the concept of moral neutrality. In describing the purposes or characteristics of actions in certain circumstances descriptions may be neutral in the sense of being objectively determinable (at least in principle), though they need not be neutral in the sense that a social scientist would have to withhold all moral judgments in determining them. According to some ethical theories this withholding would indeed be impossible, and perhaps a demand for neutrality in this strong sense has led some social theorists to see a special problem for objectivity here.[24]

A second motive for holding to anti-objectivism on the basis of some of the value arguments may be adherence to moral relativism. That is, one may confuse objectivity in social science and objectivity in morality;[25] but the two are different. It is not requisite for the objectivist position that the social scientist's value judgments be objectively decidable. Two social scientists may confront exactly the same scene, one morally condemn some aspect of it, and the other not, and it may be the case (though I am inclined to think otherwise) that the issue between them is not objectively decidable. But what is required for objectivism is only that they can objectively agree on the (non-value) characteristics of the scene.

It may be that in seeking for value-neutral language (in restricting descriptive language to the characteristics which at least accompany morally praiseworthy or blameworthy actions for the various inquirers concerned without expressing their moral views) social inquirers' accounts will lose something, namely their evaluations of what is described. And several philosophers of history, including Dray and Collingwood,[26] have argued that, by losing this, the inquirers' study has lost something vital to a writing of history (and possibly they mean to extend this to all studies of man and society). But there is nothing about the objectivist's position which compels him to prescribe eliminating all evaluations from social-scientific works.

Other possible sources of appeal of the argument from values depend on philosophical considerations not related to morality or ethics. For instance, it may be argued that motives or purposes (whether morally praised or not) are not open to objective characterization. Or it may be urged that the values a social scientist holds are part of a package of general attitudes and beliefs that go to make up his *Weltanschauung*, so that two social scientists who disagree on values will probably also have different *Weltanschauungen*, and there is no possibility of agreement between such men. Such general support for anti-objectivism will be taken up in due course.

HISTORICISM

The historicist argument has its origin mainly in German idealist philosophy and is represented today by sociological followers of Karl Mannheim. It is the argument that, since no scientific inquiry is done in a vacuum but is limited by particular historical contexts, the conclusions of any scientific enterprise are also so limited. A representative historicist argument is that of Mannheim:

The historical and social genesis of an idea would only be irrelevant to its ultimate validity if the temporal and social conditions of its emergence had no effect on its content and form. If this were the case, any two periods in the history of human knowledge would only be distinguished from one another by the fact that in the earlier period certain things were still unknown and certain errors still existed which, through later knowledge, were completely corrected.[27]

Mannheim's view is, of course, that empirical study of the history of knowledge shows that this picture is false:

Today we have arrived at the point where we can see clearly that there are differences in modes of thought, not only in different historical periods but also in different cultures. Slowly it dawns upon us that not only does the content of thought change but also its categorical structure. Only very recently has it become possible to investigate the hypothesis that, in the past as well as in the present, the dominant modes of thought are supplanted by new categories when the social basis of the group, of which these thought-forms are characteristic, disintegrates or is transformed under the impact of social change.[28]

There is an obvious sense in which this historicist thesis is plausible, namely in that the problems addressed and the hypotheses which are likely to come to mind to solve them greatly depend on extra-scientific factors which vary historically. It is also plausible that in different periods of history different biases which may affect scientific inquiry have been prevalent, and that different techniques for evaluating scientific hypotheses have been employed, e.g., different experimental, deductive, and statistical techniques. But none of this could affect the possibility of objectivity. It would have to be shown that bias is inevitable and universal, i.e., necessarily a block to objectivity in any one historical period and in all periods; since, even if all inquiries about some subject-matter in one period were biased in such a way as to fail in being objective, objectivity would still be possible as long as inquirers of any other period were not biased regarding that subject-matter (even though they might be regarding other subject-matters).

So to sustain their argument historicists would have to make a stronger claim, as Mannheim suggests when he talks of 'categorical structures of thought.' Mannheim's implied argument, similar to one examined below, is that the scientific methodological tools of any age can never yield objective knowledge, since it is only by means of these very tools that their effectiveness for gaining such knowledge can be determined. He maintains:

The problem is thus made the more difficult by the fact that the very principles, in the light of which knowledge is to be criticized, are themselves found to be socially and historically conditioned.[29]

And he holds that even epistemology must be seen to be historically relative, by which he means that criteria of evidence and even 'criteria of truth' change historically.[30]

It should be noted, in the first place, that this argument is a general conceptual one, quite different from one which proceeds from historical determinism regarding scientific thinking. The latter is an empirical claim which (perhaps because it is confused with the more general one) historicists often seem to think is obviously established by the sociology and history of knowledge. The conceptual argument, if pushed, becomes at least a kind of 'scientific paradigm' or general 'categories of thought' argument of the sort to be examined later. As it stands, it is attacked by Nagel and others for being a statement of thoroughgoing scepticism which, far from being an empirical argument, purports to prove the impossibility of all knowledge, empirically based or otherwise.

Still, historicists seem to think that this argument is at least *prima facie* compelling, and is exemplified in the history of science. However I think the argument involves a serious problem for the historicist in that it fails to distinguish among different kinds of tools used in scientific activity. Clearly the following activities are not all of the same sort:

a / using the Bohr model of the atom to explain emission spectra;

b / determining intelligence by means of some intelligence test;

c / employing a spectroscope to measure emission spectra;

d / recording and collating the results of many intelligence tests.

Now a and b in this list might be said to be 'theory-dependent' since the Bohr model is a theoretical one, and the use of an intelligence test presupposes some theory defining 'intelligence' (including a behaviouristic one which would define it in terms of ability to give certain answers on the test). But c and d are different sorts of activities in that they can be carried on independently of the particular theories. Indeed the use of the spectroscope has occasioned and tested several competing theories, and, coupled with scalogram analysis, d could be employed as part of a test of the theory of intelligence in question.

The point is that a and b are not tools which test themselves. The adequacy of the Bohr model is not tested just by constructing a model; the adequacy of the supposed theory of intelligence is not tested by giving the psychologist who originated it one of his own tests. Rather they are tested by other methods which are (not only) temporally independent of the more specific ones, but also conceptually independent, since one can conceive of accurate recordings of spectroscopic observations and answers to questions on intelligence tests by men of any era, even though they may not be able to think of ways to interpret what they observe and record.

Another inadequacy in the historicist position has to do with the heterogeneity of the history of sciences. While activities of sort a and b and of sort c and d both have histories, the histories are different in kind. Changes in theories of micro-physics may be total, involving radical breaks with past theories, but the development of spectrographic analysis and the skills of mental ability testing have more or less continuous histories, each phase of which depends upon accepting some of what has gone before (e.g., spectrographic analysis depends on earlier work with prisms). I think historicists tend to mix the two kinds of activity together partly because there is one kind of historical interdependence – there would be no point in building and using spectroscopes and making up intelligence tests if there were not specific kinds of theories to be tested, and partly because some theory or other is needed for the interpretation of observations. But to support his case the historicist would have to show that both kinds of 'tools' stand or fall together, and more or less simultaneously; this seems historically false.

In addition to citing historical differences of perspective in defense of his theory, Mannheim also mentions differences among 'social group-ings' within one historical period, usually in connection with his (guarded) praise of Marxism as a major forerunner of his own general position in the sociology of knowledge,[31] and it is not uncommon today to hear people who (unlike Mannheim) on the whole endorse Marxism espousing the same view. But such an addition in no way strengthens the historicist position. That any theorist has class-based value commit-ments or factual beliefs (or those based on any other social or political position) does not *prove* that he cannot arrive at (objectively) true con-clusions or that there cannot be some continuity of scientific conclusions and tools of inquiry from class to class as from historical epoch to histori-cal epoch, even though there may also be irreconcilable differences in the willingness or even ability of some to use certain tools or arrive at certain conclusions.

It is noteworthy that Marx himself, far from espousing the anti-objectivism attributed to him by many modern historicists, at one point praised Ricardo for sometimes coming to 'scientifically honest' and 'scientifically necessary' conclusions which were at variance with the class interests usually favoured by Ricardo.[32] And in one of the few places where he might be interpreted to be relating his history and sociology of knowledge to the possibility of objectivity, Marx seems to adhere to the view that some social conditions are conducive to objec-tive inquiry, while others are not.[33] Also Lenin, as is well known, devoted much of his philosophical writings to attacking relativism, while still holding that knowledge is relative 'not in the sense of the denial of objective truth, but in the sense of the historically conditional nature of the limits of the approximation of our knowledge of this truth.'[34]

The expression of objectivist views by Marx and Lenin seems to me especially noteworthy since they point up a typically mistaken orienta-tion of anti-objectivists employing historicism. Agreeing with arguments to show that social conditions determine the kinds of theoretical prob-lems addressed and the likelihood of arriving at either false and distorted or (only more or less) adequate conclusions, historicists seem to think that therefore all methods and conclusions are suspect. That is, they suppose an undefended dichotomy between inquiry being carried on completely unconditioned by social, economic, etc., factors on the one hand and objective inquiry being impossible on the other – a supposition not, apparently, shared by some of the very men whose theories on the history of ideas are taken to be among the origins of this anti-objectivist position.

THE ARGUMENT FROM SELECTION

The argument from selection (or it might also be called the one from classification) is represented, with hints of almost all its supporting arguments, by Gunnar Myrdal:

Scientific facts do not exist *per se*, waiting to be discovered by scientists. A scientific fact is a construction abstracted from a complex and interwoven reality by means of arbitrary definitions and classifications. The processes of selecting a problem and a basic hypothesis, of limiting the scope of the study, and of defining and classifying data relevant to such a setting of the problem involve a choice on the part of the investigator. The choice is made from an indefinite number of possibilities.[35]

This argument can be conjoined with general theories about language and perception, or it can be advanced as an independent argument to the effect that the need for classification alone makes objectivity impossible. But while the latter form of the argument is the one most often advanced by anti-objectivists, it does not seem to me to pose a serious threat to the objectivist position.

While it is true that scientists must select certain subject-matters, and classify elements of those subject-matters, this in no way by itself supports anti-objectivism, as is evidenced by the fact that, while it is not usual to speak of systems of classification as objective or not objective, debates about the adequacy of such systems are not uncommon in most sciences, and these debates often turn on whether a theory using one system of classification is more or less successful at yielding (objectively) true hypotheses than one using another. It seems at least *prima facie* true (and in its blatant form this argument purports to proceed from *prima facie* truths) that some recognition of the features of things is possible independently of beliefs based on some theory to be tested (including the theory's classificatory system) in the same way that it seemed possible to recognize features of something independently of moral views in order to make moral judgments about it. It may be that typological work supposes having some theory, and does not proceed just inductively, and this might be what leads some anti-objectivists to think that the need for classification and selection obviously supports their view. But, as has been noted, objectivism does not commit one to inductivism.

Accordingly some anti-objectivists who employ the argument from selection give supporting arguments. One, to be found in the writings of Max Weber and others,[36] appeals to the infinity of aspects of things. If nature (human or otherwise) is limitlessly complex and therefore capable of being described in limitless ways, then the need for selecting *which* of these ways is supposed to support anti-objectivism. Clearly it does not: what is at issue is whether what is selected can be objectively described and explained.

A related argument proceeds from the infinite possibility of law-like description. Thus Michael Polanyi, in an argument which applies only to quantitatively expressible laws, presumably the strong point of objectivity for him, writes:[37]

There are many forms of mathematical series ... each of which can be used in an infinite variety of fashions to approximate the existing data to any desired degree. Never yet has a definite rule been laid down by which any particular mathematical function can be recognized, among the infinite number of those offering themselves for choice, as the one which expresses a natural law.

This argument is essentially the same as that of Leach discussed above and can be met in the same ways. In fact in his very next sentence Polanyi himself gives a rule for making objective choice:

It is true that each of the infinite number of available functions will, in general, lead to a different prediction when applied to new observations, but this does not provide the requisite test for making a selection among them. If we pick out those which predict rightly, we still have an infinite number on our hands.

Polanyi's reference to the possibility of infinitely closer description does not disqualify predictive power as a rule for objective selection (unless the view that to know anything one must know everything is adopted). If theory A can be objectively known to be more accurate than theory B, since compared to B it is in closer accord with the facts, as is revealed by its superior predictive power, then this can be objectively known even if some other theory, C, happens to be even more in accord with the facts. What seems to worry Polanyi is that not only may there be theories more in accord with the facts, but at any stage of description there will be theories just as in accord. But why should this pose a problem? Either future descriptions will again prove some of these objectively better than others (by tending to verify the theories of which they are parts) or not, and, if not, other principles of selection (like simplicity and scope) may be employed, but the possibility of (objective) correction will always remain.

Polanyi might want to extend his argument one step further and urge that, since no theory is ever absolutely determined by exclusively empirical considerations, it is possible that opposing theories could be equally supported by the results of all possible observational tests and that extra-empirical considerations might themselves presuppose theories (e.g., about the history of science), which theories could again share with rivals consonance with all possible empirical facts; so a regress would be generated. The problem with this is that a regress is indeed generated, a sceptical regress. If arguments based on such (mere) possibilities are given weight, then so too must arguments proceeding from such possibilities as that there might be equal support for rival theories about the relationship between theories and data in science or the use of empirical and extra-empirical considerations. The problem with trying to strengthen Polanyi's support for the argument from selection in this way is in avoiding thoroughgoing scepticism of the kind discussed in chapter 2 in connection with some of Thomas Kuhn's views. The difficulty of solving this problem will be seen to be greater than some anti-objectivists suppose.

A third kind of support is suggested by the frequent use by anti-objectivists of the word 'category' as a synonym for 'classification.' It is a Kant-like argument that when we embark on an inquiry we employ certain schemata in such a way that the conclusions of the inquiry can never reveal the nature of its subject-matter as it is, but only as predetermined by these schemata. Cicourel and Hayek often argue something like this as a psychological theory.[38] For example, Cicourel argues that our classifications are all made in accord with 'common sense categories.' But in the first place, it is hard to see what these anti-objectivists think could psychologically dispose us to see facts in certain ways other than such factors as the historically conditioned biases already discussed. Moreover the appeal to common sense can be confronted with the historical counter-example that science has often challenged and changed the views of common sense. And in the second place, as has been noted, systems of classification, like stipulative definitions, are not objective or non-objective, though their use in theories may be helpful or not in generating (objectively) true or false hypotheses; and so the charge as a psychological one does not militate against objectivism. The mere psychological fact that systems of classification are historically conditioned does not prove or disprove the possibility of objectivity.

Others, like Polanyi, have advanced this argument as a philosophical doctrine. Thus Polanyi claims that the categories of common sense are 'logically anterior' to those of any science, since it is in common sense that the facts of any science are determined.[39] This view, if it could be supported by anti-objectivists would challenge objectivism, since it would claim that no subject-matter is ever accessible as it actually is but can only be accessible as predetermined by some anterior schemata which provide the scientist's system of classification; and if the schemata could (even in principle) differ from scientist to scientist, so that some scientists were addressing facts interpreted in one way, others in another, and no objective decision between them could be reached, then anti-objectivism would indeed follow.

OBJECTIVISM AND ANTI-OBJECTIVISM

What is especially noteworthy about this move of the anti-objectivist – employing the argument from selection – is that it is also a move open to anti-objectivists using historicism and the argument from values.

So at the end of his discussion of objectivity and value Abraham Kaplan writes: '... values enter both into making the prediction and into the conceptualization of what "it" is being predicted,'[40] where the quotation marks around the word 'it' are supposed to indicate that values predetermine the nature of the subject-matter under consideration; and Mannheim writes:

Every epoch has its fundamentally new approach and its characteristic point of view, and consequently sees the 'same' object from a new perspective.[41]

The quotation marks in this passage are meant to indicate the same view as those in Kaplan's.

The argument which all three kinds of defences of anti-objectivism seek support in are versions of the general view that descriptions and explanations of a subject-matter cannot be objectively accepted, rejected, or altered, since the means of testing an inquirer's conclusions (including both his perceptions and whatever extra-empirical criteria he employs) are somehow determined by theories about the subject-matter already held by him (perhaps unconsciously). Anti-objectivists often make the point that all facts are 'theory-laden' in some strong sense such that reference to facts cannot guide one in deciding among rival theories.

Perhaps examples of the position will make clearer what is meant by anti-objectivists here:[42]

... paradigm changes do cause scientists to see the world of their research-engagement differently. In so far as their only recourse to that world is through what they see and do, we may want to say that after a scientific revolution scientists are responding to a different world.   THOMAS KUHN

Since almost all sociological measurement ... is arbitrary, we cannot afford to ignore the three media – language, cultural meanings, and properties of measurement systems – through which we formulate theoretically derived or *ad hoc* categories and link them with observable properties of objects and events ... Each of the three media acts as a 'grid' for defining and letting certain forms of 'data' through to the observer. Each 'grid' becomes a 'filter' for what we come to perceive and interpret as its referent, its significance, and its logical status as a datum. Each 'grid' or medium shapes or influences our perception and interpretation of our common-sense and scientific experiences.   A.V. CICOUREL

It is simply irrelevant to criticize earlier scientists for blindness, when the doctrines they failed to accept had no intelligible place within the theoretical framework of their time. If they sometimes seem to us now to have shut their eyes to the facts, we need to ask: 'Could these things which we regard as "facts" have been certain, clear, or even intelligible to earlier investigators?' The continual interaction of theory with fact – the way in which theories are built on facts, while at the same time giving significance to them and even determining what are 'facts' for us at all: that ... is the extraordinary fascination and delight to be had from reflecting on the historical evolution of scientific ideas.   STEPHEN TOULMIN

... scientific theories are ways of looking at the world; and their adoption affects our general beliefs and expectations, and thereby also our experiences and our conception of reality. We may even say that what is regarded as 'nature' at a particular time is our own product in the sense that all the features ascribed to it have first been invented by us and then used for bringing order into our surroundings.   P.K. FEYERABEND

Advocates of this view have been criticized for not defining 'theory,' but they seem to mean by the term either the common sense categories and doctrines embedded in everyday discourse (as Cicourel argues) or one's personal *Weltanschauung*, the very general principles he uses for interpreting his experiences. Or the term might be used in a narrow sense to refer to a body of laws and definitions which explain why the regularities expressed in laws of observation hold – although it will be pointed out that in some anti-objectivist views there could be only an arbitrary distinction between observation and theoretical laws.

Also the word 'fact' is notoriously slippery in philosophical circles. One argument (unobjectionable in itself) would even make it analytic that facts are in some sense 'theory-laden.' Employing a definition of a 'fact' as 'what a true statement states,' which would distinguish facts, as having to do with the descriptions of things, events, and states, from the things, events, and states described, it might then be urged that facts, being linguistic in nature, are all necessarily 'laden' with theories at least as reflected in the language used in description.[43]

For it to be more than a merely verbal quibble an argument proceeding from this definition would have to be part of a general position regarding the relation of language to experience, like those discussed in chapter 3. However the various uses of 'fact' need not detain us. Suffice it to note that for the anti-objectivist to say that 'facts' are 'theory-laden' or are 'determined' by one's theory is to say that how an inquirer *could* experience, contemplate, or describe a subject-matter is predetermined by the theories that he holds (however vaguely or unconsciously).

It is apparent that the correctness of this view would provide support for the anti-objectivist arguments discussed above. Hence Israel Scheffler devotes his book *Science and Subjectivity*, which defends objectivism in natural science, to this theory; and Richard Rudner, usually a defender of objectivism, sees a problem for the objectivist when positions in the philosophy of language bearing on this theory-ladenness view are taken into account.[44] If the theories one holds determine what his perceptions and interpretations of things described by the theories can be, so that his adoption or abandonment of a theory cannot depend on his recognition of qualities and relations of the things concerned, then it would be plausible to argue that their adoption or abandonment is dependent on his values or non-scientific circumstances of his historical period. And insofar as classification is on the basis of some theory, the theory would *ipso facto* determine one's perceptions and interpretations of what is classified.

Accordingly different grounds must be found for this theory-ladenness view itself. I find four kinds of grounds: one defence purporting to be based on the nature and history of science, one from the nature of language, one from the nature of perception, and several arguments from the special nature of the social-scientific subject-matters. The first three of these apply to all scientific inquiry, and it seems to me desirable to take these into account. Arguments which are often inadequately presented as applied just to anti-objectivism in social science are better developed in their more general applications. Also critics of anti-objectivism often defend objectivism in social science by showing that objectivity is possible there if it is possible in non-social sciences, leaving open the anti-objectivist rejoinder that it is possible in neither.

However recent work suggests that an excursion through these arguments is unnecessary, since the anti-objectivist position is faced with an irreconcilable conflict from the very start, no matter what arguments are turned to for support, whether of the variety discussed below, or any of those discussed above. For the anti-objectivist a theory somehow determines the nature of what one can experience; and hence cannot be refuted (or objectively supported) by reference to experience. Scheffler has ferreted what he calls 'paradoxes' out of this position, two of which have also been noted by other critics of anti-objectivism.[45]

One of these is that, if the position were correct, then no two theories of sufficient generality could ever really disagree, since they could not be said to be purporting to explain the same things; the other, a particularly damaging species of the first, is that no proponent of this position, itself part of a theory (about the relation of experience to theories), could consistently claim that a position which contradicts his own is false while his is true. These are not properly paradoxes (though in the case of a rational man who understands the second a pragmatic contradiction may be involved) as much as they are unhappy consequences of the anti-objectivist's position. The question is whether the anti-objectivist can accept these consequences.

In fact anti-objectivists are willing to accept the first consequence and admit that it is not on the bases of factual confirmation or disconfimation that one theory is abandoned for another. Indeed some do not even seem to see this as an *unhappy* consequence, since it affords historians and philosophers of science a continual drama of extra-rationally motivated scientific revolutions. The second consequence, however, might be more difficult to accept. If, as I think can be argued, sincerely to believe a theory is to believe that it is objectively true, then the second consequence of the anti-objectivist position would be that he would have to admit either that he does not believe his theory or that it is objectively true; neither alternative would be attractive to him. If he does not believe the view, why does he advocate it? If *it* is objectively true, why cannot *other* theories also be objectively true? The burden would lie on the anti-objectivist to show what there is about his endeavour (e.g., its generality, or its specifically philosophical or meta-scientific nature) that allows it and it alone to escape his own anti-objectivist claim (and he would have to show this without himself employing or supposing the conclusions of any theory the objectivity of which he has tried to show impossible).

It has sometimes seemed to me, as to other objectivists, that such considerations are sufficient to dispose of anti-objectivism. However anti-objectivists themselves have been singularly undaunted by this most general objection to their view. Possibly this is because they think that particular arguments in favour of anti-objectivism are so strong that there must be something wrong with the self-defeating argument. Accordingly it will be instructive to go through representative defences of anti-objectivism to indicate that considerations which have apparently made this position attractive to many involve serious problems; and in addition an opportunity will be afforded to sketch an objectivist position opposed to it.

CHAPTER TWO

The nature and history of science

THEORIES AND EXPLANATIONS

Many arguments for anti-objectivism purporting to be based on the nature of scientific description and explanation hinge on arguments in the philosophies of language and perception and are better discussed in later chapters; however there are some defences of this position which claim to show that theory and fact are so related in scientific inquiry that the one cannot be independent of the other in the way required by objectivism. Some of these arguments are more plausible, at least initially, than others, but I think they all fail primarily because they take a simplistic view of the enterprise of scientific explanation.

One argument appeals to the criteria for testing a theory. Thus at one time Mary Hesse argued:

... if phenomenal statements are to be tests of a theory, they cannot be independent of the theory ... The conditions given for phenomenal statements are not sufficient for them to have scientific significance, and if they are to have such significance, there must be connections of meaning between them at a higher than common-sense level, and therefore the condition of complete theoretical independence between them must be dropped.[1]

The article in which this passage appears is directed against what is called the 'dictionary theory,' which sometimes seems to refer to the view that the terms of any theory can be given meaning only by translating them into terms understood prior to any scientific theory, and at other times to the view that they can only be given meaning by translating them into sense-datum language (though perhaps she would hold that these come to the same thing).

At any rate the argument is either harmless to the objectivist position or unsound (depending on what is meant by phrases like 'independent of the theory' and 'connections of meaning'). This is evidenced, as one critic points out,[2] by the fact that statements of fact are often quite well understood long before theories explaining those facts are found. On one interpretation of the view this would just mean that it must be possible to find some way that the terms of these antecedently understood descriptive statements can be made sense of in a theory which purports to explain the facts; on another interpretation it would mean that only theories which accidentally shared terms with the same meanings as those in the descriptions could have explained such facts (a highly improbable state of affairs).

One line of escape for this argument in the spirit of anti-objectivism would be to say that statements of fact understood antecedently to some theory are determined by another theory which is, so to speak, tangent to that which purports to explain the facts (in that at least some of the terms of the two theories are the same or are straightforwardly inter-definable). But the problem with this is to show why, if observation statements can thus be common to two theories, they cannot be common to an indefinite number of (actual or possible) theories, so long as these are (directly or indirectly) tangent to one another. As long as the anti-objectivist rests his case on the mere fact that a theory's descriptions are in the language of the theory, I do not see how he can rule this out; but if he admits this he admits that, while it may be that to describe something is to describe it in the language of a theory (perhaps including common sense theories of everyday life), he can place no upper limit on the factual descriptions which can be shared by any number of rival theories.

This attempt at defending anti-objectivism is instructive. It indicates that an argument for the theory-ladenness of facts is not proven just by *prima facie* appeal to scientific explanations; such arguments must be buttressed by special analyses of these explanations. One more or less popular analysis has to do with what might be called the scope and internal organization of theories. Theories, it is urged, are much more general than empirical generalizations, and the terms of theories are given meaning by the theory itself, by explicit definition or by the roles the terms play within theories. From this it is supposed to follow that the facts 'explained' by a theory cannot occasion or contribute to verification of the theory, since the generality of the theory is such as to accommodate facts very differently interpreted. Nor can the recognition of some facts rationally compel someone to replace one theory with another, since the meanings of the terms of each theory are determined within those theories. I think that it is considerations like these which led Toulmin to the conclusion quoted above, but this view is more fully set forth by

P.K. Feyerabend in his important article 'Explanation, Reduction, and Empiricism.'[3]

In this article, as elsewhere, Feyerabend argues that replacing one theory with another involves 'a complete replacement of the ontology' of the one with that of the other, with a 'corresponding change of the meanings' of its descriptive terms, and that as a result

... introducing a new theory involves changes of outlook both with respect to the observable and with respect to the unobservable features of the world, and corresponding changes in the meanings of even the most 'fundamental' terms of the language employed.[4]

Most of Feyerabend's arguments for this hinge on positions in the philosophies of language and perception and will be examined in due course, but he does offer an argument which might profitably be examined here. He argues that if the positions opposed to his were correct, then it must be possible that:

(A) reduction or explanation is (or should be) by derivation;
(B) the meanings of (observational) terms are invariant with respect to both reduction and explanation.[5]

By A Feyerabend means that a theory must either 'contain' as logical consequences all facts it is to explain or at least be 'consistent' with them; by B he means that, if two theories purport to explain the same facts, it must be possible to define terms which refer to such facts in one theory by means of terms in the other. Without these principles two scientists holding rival theories could never, so to speak, square off in such a way as to make objective decision between them possible. Without what Feyerabend calls 'derivation' no theorist would be committed to any consequence of his theory, and without 'meaning invariance' it would be impossible for two scientists to express conflicting consequences of their theories in the same language, so no statement of consequences which are clearly rivals would be possible.

Now Feyerabend's main arguments against A are:

... that one and the same set of observational data is compatible with very different and mutually inconsistent theories. This is possible for two reasons: first, because theories, which are universal, always go beyond any set of observations that might be available at any particular time: second, because the truth of an observation statement can always be asserted within a certain margin of error only.[6]

To argue against B Feyerabend adduces a counter-example (much laboured by him and by other anti-objectivists). This is that 'the concept of impetus, as fixed by the usage established in the impetus theory, cannot be defined in a reasonable way within Newton's theory.'[7] Feyerabend's argument for this is that the Newtonian concept of momentum plays the same role in Newton's theory that impetus does in the earlier one, but 'impetus' cannot be translated as 'momentum,' or any other word in Newton's theory, since the concept of impetus involves the concept of a force which exerts a kind of pushing or pulling on bodies, just the kind of concept the new science was concerned to abandon.

It should be noted at the outset that, as they stand, these arguments have serious problems. Regarding his first argument against A, of course theories 'go beyond any set of observations'; this follows from their being composed of laws rather than summaries. What is at issue is whether future observations can or cannot tend to support some theories and disconfirm others; just to assert that they cannot begs the central question. Regarding the second argument against A, it has often been pointed out that the mere fact that a law may hold only approximately does not show that the *explanandum* of that law cannot be explained by reference to it – in conjunction with other laws.[8] In any but a closed and very limited system, where 'perfect knowledge' is available, it will be the case that laws will hold only approximately. But this does not mean that those laws can be made to accommodate any facts, and, indeed, when imperfection of knowledge is adduced to account for apparent failure of a law to hold, the apparent counter-instance is not always somehow made to fit a law of the theory which holds only approximately, but is also explained by reference to some other (actual or possible) law(s) of the entire theory.

Feyerabend's arguments against B are even less convincing. In the first place, neither 'impetus' nor 'force' is an observation term, and on Feyerabend's view it is the meanings of observation terms that must be invariant for the objectivist position to be upheld. In the second place, if 'impetus' means 'something which causes something else to move by pushing it,' then it could not be defined as 'momentum,' in part because the Newtonian theory was concerned to replace concepts like 'impetus' so defined with very different ones in order better to explain regularities in the motions of things. But certainly 'impetus' could be defined in terms which any Newtonian could understand and could, if he saw any point in doing so, incorporate into his formal theory (e.g., 'a push').

Several characteristics of Feyerabend's argument are noteworthy for present purposes. One is that it is typical of anti-objectivist arguments from the nature of scientific explanation in that it places unwarrantedly restrictive demands on explanations and the acceptable conceptual relations among competing theories. Like many anti-objectivist arguments, this one seems to rest on a false dichotomy : either perfect (non-approximate) knowledge is possible and competing theories can easily be compared by something like straightforward inter-definition of all their terms, or objectivity is an ideal never to be achieved. But why must this be the case? As I see it, there is an all too often unacknowledged burden here for the anti-objectivist of defending this dichotomy, since the objectivist position seems supported by the examples of successful scientific (and everyday) practice based on probabilistic explanations and explanations which yield only approximately true conclusions and by close examination of specific scientific-theoretical controversies like the one cited by Feyerabend.[9]

Another interesting feature of Feyerabend's argument is that it links an attack on objectivism with an attack on what is sometimes called the deductive-nomological model of scientific explanation, that is, on the view that (in the ideal case) scientifically to explain an event or state is to deduce a report of its occurrence or existence from the statement of some law (in conjunction with statements of antecedant conditions). Now it is not at all obvious that the stand one takes on the deductivist view of scientific explanation commits him to a stand on objectivism. A deductivist might advocate anti-objectivism (possibly Poincaré is an example). Also an anti-deductivist could remain an objectivist at least regarding description; and Carl Hempel, the most famous defender of the deductivist view, is an objectivist regarding at least one non-deductive sort of explanation.

But, more importantly, the deductive-nomological view is not, as many of its opponents and some of its supporters seem to assume, a philosophical thesis in answer to the question of what constitutes *evidence*; and hence the deductivist view is not (at least directly) about the question of objectivity. The view is, rather, a philosophical theory about the nature of scientific *explanation*. Hence Hempel is prepared to admit that a scientist can be (objectively) justified in drawing some conclusion as regards the explanation of something, even though, as in the case of his 'statistical-nomological' explanations, he cannot state it as the conclusion of a deductive argument. Disputes can be carried on about just what has been explained in such cases and about the mechanics of statistical explanations, but these disputes are about explanation, not about objectivity, despite the tendency of some to confuse the two issues.[10]

However, the correctness of the anti-objectivist position, no matter how defended, might be a plausible (if not welcome) support for some interpretations of scientific explanation; and in any case the objectivist will be comfortable and the anti-objectivist uncomfortable with the deductive model. If a theory T is a system of laws by means of which a kind of fact f can be explained (by deduction), then if f were unidentifiable independently of T, the deduction of (descriptions of) f from (statements of) T would, in a sense, be pointless. For the objectivist, on the other hand, f, identifiable in advance of any of a number of theories which might explain it, would serve as a kind of base or guide for explanation. First f is identified; then various laws by reference to which it might be explained are sought. The difference is that, in the case of the objectivist, there is a clear conceptual line between identifying an *explanandum* and discovering an *explanans*, while for at least many anti-objectivists there is not. Accordingly it is not surprising that the anti-objectivist is more at home with a model of scientific explanation in which coming to identify an *explanandum* is somehow part of the same process as 'discovering' an *explanans*. Once such a process has been completed, it would, of course, be possible to go ahead and derive the *explanandum* from the *explanans* by deduction, but it would be pointless. Thus critics of the deductive-nomological view as it is supposed to apply to history point out that deductive formulations of historical explanation, in addition to being trivial, are superfluous.

It is because the deductivist model is more confortably held by the objectivist than by his opponent that anti-objectivists sometimes frame their attacks on objectivism as attacks on deductivism and reject this model of explanation. Rather they tend to adopt the view that to explain something is to 'fit it into a pattern,' where that pattern is not a deductive system, but one's general way of looking at things, his 'tradition' or the 'metaphysics' of his time. The guiding principles of such patterns are not laws but something more vague, often called 'paradigms.'

Another interesting feature of Feyerabend's arguments is that they rest at some point on empirical claims: that laws in science have failed to hold in any way but approximately, and that at least one theory has replaced another without its adherents being able to define the terms of the earlier one. Indeed it is the dependence on such claims which has led critics of Feyerabend to emphasize the susceptibility of his view to the self-defeating aspect of anti-objectivist positions. These two features of Feyerabend's arguments – the criticism of the deductive-nomological model of scientific explanation with the concomitant sympathy for a paradigm-guided pattern model, and an appeal to the actual history of science – have been the main components of most recent arguments given for anti-objectivism purporting to be based on an examination of the enterprise of scientific inquiry itself.

PARADIGMS

One reason that some philosophers of science have been suspicious of what is here called the pattern model of scientific explanation is that, unlike the deductive one, the pattern model is so vague as to be almost useless for the purpose of explicating scientific explanation. To describe scientific explanation as 'fitting' facts into a 'framework' or 'making sense' of them seems to do justice to the complexity of scientific inquiry only because such descriptions are so vague as to admit of many interpretations. This same vagueness attaches to the concepts of the paradigms which are supposed to guide such explanation, but on any of several interpretations it can still be shown that the analysis of scientific inquiry by means of these paradigm concepts fails to support the anti-objectivist position.

In his influential book *The Structure of Scientific Revolutions* Thomas Kuhn introduces the theory of paradigms by listing several examples of scientific treatises which were[11]

sufficiently unprecedented to attract an enduring group of adherents away from competing modes of scientific activity ... [and] sufficiently open-ended to leave all sorts of problems for the redefined group of practitioners to resolve.

These works are ones which have set new paradigms for subsequent scientific inquiry:

Achievements that share these two characteristics I shall henceforth refer to as 'paradigms,' a term that relates closely to 'normal science.' By choosing it, I mean to suggest that some accepted examples of actual scientific practice – examples which include law, theory, application, and instrumentation together – provide models from which spring particular coherent traditions of scientific research. These are the traditions which the historian describes under such rubrics as 'Ptolemaic astronomy' (or 'Copernican'), 'Aristotelian dynamics' (or 'Newtonian'), 'corpuscular optics' (or 'wave optics'), and so on.

Sharing a paradigm is following some such 'model,' and Kuhn, echoing a common argument against objectivism, which might be called the 'paradox of paradigm evaluation,' maintains that anti-objectivism regarding the paradigms themselves is implied by the fact that all scientists follow them:

When paradigms enter, as they must, into a debate about paradigm choice, their role is necessarily circular. Each group uses its own paradigm to argue in that paradigm's defense.[12]

Kuhn includes, as parts of a paradigm, laws, theories, application, and instrumentation 'together'; so a scientist's paradigm would seem to be the whole of that scientist's theory as well as the methods he uses to substantiate it. This view is shared by some other anti-objectivists; for example, I think Toulmin supposes it when he writes that it is 'irrelevant to criticize earlier scientists for blindness, when the doctrines they failed to accept had no intelligible place within the theoretical framework of their time,'[13] as does S.F. Nadel when he speaks of a 'system' as the 'reasoning underlying observation and description.'[14]

One criticism (mentioned above) of this blanket interpretation of paradigms raised by Scheffler and Dudley Shapere[15] among others is that, if it were true, then two different paradigms could never properly be said to be competing, since each would be determining its own facts and the methods and concepts which would figure in deciding among paradigms. An anti-objectivist's reaction to this charge is likely to be that it does not adversely effect his position. He may agree that two theories never really compete, and hold that, instead, theories just as a matter of fact replace one another. The effect of such an argument (inasmuch as it hinges on a particular view of sense and reference) will be examined in the next chapter, but the all-encompassing nature of paradigms in this view, which gives rise to the consequence pointed out be Scheffler and Shapere, also leads to another nest of difficulties which may be more damaging to the anti-objectivist position.

Suppose that a scientist 'working within' a paradigm P is confronted with an hypothesis H as a candidate for being a theoretical law. How is he to decide whether to accept H? The anti-objectivist holds that at least one desideratum will be how well H accounts for observed events as determined by P.[16] But in the view now under consideration P just *is* a sum total of laws, definitions, and methodological principles held by the members of any one scientific 'tradition.' This means that, were H to become a law, the character of P and of the facts P addresses would change; so to decide whether to admit H would also be to make some decision about P. However it seems detrimental to the anti-objectivist's position to admit this, since we are supposed somehow to be locked within paradigms; and if he admits we can make decisions which change them, he admits we are not locked within them. Possible escapes from this difficulty result in futher problems for the anti-objectivist.

One line of escape is to make distinctions among the different elements of a paradigm in such a way that some elements can be admitted (or deleted) without changing the paradigm. However it is hard to see how any such distinction can be maintained. It cannot, of course, be urged that the facts of a paradigm are constant, and that it is against them that other elements are measured, since this is tantamount to abandoning anti-objectivism. Nor can the anti-objectivist argue that the distinction is to be between theoretical and observational laws, since in his position there can be only an arbitrary distinction between them. If the anti-objectivist attempts to set up a hierarchy of theoretical laws and definitions such that a top portion of them are ones which define the paradigm and determine what hypotheses are to be accepted, or if he attempts to make some classificatory scheme perform this function, then he runs into a species of the same problem as before. What is he to do with proposals to alter the top of the hierarchy of the classificatory scheme, since to decide on them is again to decide on the paradigm?

Another possible escape is to admit that decisions can be made about paradigms, but deny that such decisions can be rational in the sense that they involve objectivity. The argument now goes that the facts of one paradigm P_1 are determined by that paradigm and the facts of another P_2 are determined by it, and if a scientist has decided to abandon the theories of P_1 for those of P_2 or any other paradigm, his decision cannot be based on P_2's ability to account for its facts, since it determines them, but must be extra-objectively decided.

However a kind of objectivity will still be admitted by the anti-objectivist, the objectivity within each paradigm. So the report of some observed regularity O_1 may be true in P_1, but not in P_2; whereas another report O_2, offered in circumstances similar to those in which it would be appropriate to give O_1 for an adherent of P_1 (assuming some criterion of being in similar circumstances could be given), may be 'objectively' true in P_2. This being so, we may ask whether O_1 and O_2 report the same fact. The anti-objectivist cannot say that they do, because, if they did, P_1 and P_2 would just be different ways of expressing the same facts.

The difficulty in taking this view has often been noted by critics of anti-objectivism; what is not often noted, however, is that the anti-objectivist also meets difficulties if he takes the other view, that O_1 and O_2 do *not* report the same facts. If they do not, if they report two different facts, then what is to prevent someone from introducing a third paradigm P_3 which would have O_1 and O_2 as reports of facts to be explained objectively within P3? As long as the anti-objectivist's appeal is only to the nature and history of science, he cannot rule out the possibility of some common 'paradigm' being found for all such cases.[17]

A second interpretation of paradigms is also to be found in Kuhn when he talks of them as 'the source of the methods, problem-field, and standards of solution accepted by any mature scientific community at any given time.'[18] Earlier Kuhn linked this view of paradigms with what has here been called the 'paradox of paradigm evaluation.'[19] In these passages he seems to interpret a paradigm as a criterion for deciding what a problem for any scientific inquiry is and what would count as a solution. This is what makes it impossible for any two scientists to come to a rational agreement; they can never agree about the solutions to problems, or even about the problems, since the criteria necessary for coming to agreement differ. In such cases, according to Kuhn, the only recourse is 'to external criteria that most obviously make paradigm debates revolutionary.'[20]

A problem with this interpretation of paradigms seems to me that it can be pushed either into a position only trivially different from objectivism or into a thoroughgoing scepticism which, if true, would make all science as well as all philosophy and history of science (including Kuhn's) impossible. Considering the way Kuhn defines 'normal science,' his assertion that one must abandon paradigms in order to change the course of normal science is trivially true.[21] What he seems to mean is that any one scientific theory (or interrelated group of theories) somehow sets criteria which determine what it is rational to attempt to solve and what it is rational to accept or reject in the way of solutions, so that to criticize these theories as a whole one would have to employ some other criteria.

Now the obvious questions to ask are, first, why the criteria of one theory cannot be such as to allow a scientist using them to see that none of his solutions are adequate, and second, why the adopting of new criteria cannot itself be objectively carried out. To be sure, criteria of the kind Kuhn has in mind are not susceptible of being objective in the same way as scientific laws or descriptions, but they can be said to be objective to the extent that a scientist using or supposing them is able thereby to conduct (objectively) fruitful scientific inquiry, and failing in this endeavour may (objectively) turn to other criteria. Indeed challenging the objective adequacy of a scientific theory is often challenging its limits (as when modern physicists challenged the unrestricted range of application of classical mechanics, or biochemists dispute over what is to count as living).

The problem then for an anti-objectivist argument proceeding out of this kind of paradigm analysis is in showing that paradigms as criteria are not themselves susceptible of objective evaluation. I see no argument short of a general argument about the nature of criteria of objective evaluation itself. I am thinking of the classic sceptical argument of Sextus Empiricus that rational acceptance or rejection of any theory or view requires some criterion, but then rational evaluation of a criterion would always either be circular or generate an infinite regress. But surely the anti-objectivist would not want to resort to this, first because it is not without problems of its own (e.g., it assumes without warrant on its own grounds that there can never be a self-evidently correct criterion), but primarily because, if the argument were sound, it would necessitate a thoroughgoing scepticism, so no opinion could ever be rationally justified (including those of the sceptics) – a position which nobody has or could ever sincerely hold.

A defence of anti-objectivism which appeals to a third possible interpretation of paradigms, included in the first passage quoted from Kuhn above, is that paradigms are canons of scientific method. 'Scientific method' can be taken in either a narrow or a broad sense, and, while it is not always clear which sense Kuhn has in mind, neither will support anti-objectivism. In a narrow sense there are different and developing scientific methods, because there are different and developing scientific theories addressing themselves to different problems. Different methods are necessary to produce typologies, to pursue deductive work, and to pursue inductive work; and as a science develops new methodological tools (e.g., statistical techniques in sociology) are required. Moreover different scientific theories, for instance, Parsonian action theory or game theory in social science, require different methods for their testing and application. But in this narrow sense differences in scientific method are compatible with one another and with rival scientific theories using them, so it is hard to see how they can be paradigms determining different subject-matters.

In a postscript to the second edition of his book Kuhn, meeting the charges of his critics, interprets paradigms in a way that might classify them as parts of scientific method, as examples of scientific problem-solving techniques. Kuhn argues that, just as a student often figures out how to solve a complex problem in a textbook by finding some similarity between it and an earlier, exemplary one, so in the history of science scientists 'solve puzzles by modeling them on previous puzzle solutions,' and he gives the example of modifications of Newton's second law of motion made in order to apply it to pendulums and harmonic oscillators as well as to bodies in free fall.[22] Undoubtedly scientists do look for such similarities, but this fact alone does not militate against the position of objectivism, since what is at issue is whether or not it is possible to arrive at and sustain laws which might serve as examples, and to determine whether there are sufficient (objective) similarities to use them fruitfully as examples.

Kuhn, in fact, does develop this interpretation of paradigms by arguing that, in employing a problem-solving model, a scientist tacitly accepts criteria of what is to count as similar to it (though for Kuhn 'criteria' is a misleading word, since the 'recognition of similarity may also be involuntary').[23] However, in addition to its being dubious that employing some example does commit one in the way Kuhn holds, this argument is essentially the same as the paradox of paradigm evaluation argument, with the same sceptical consequences.[24]

Taken in a broad sense, the scientific method (or at least the core of the many methods employed from science to science and over time in one science) may be seen by the objectivist as itself being an attempt to organize inquiry in such a way as to gain objective conclusions about various subject-matters. And so to assert that the scientific method in this broad sense is a paradigm which makes scientific objectivity impossible is just to assert one's adherence to anti-objectivism, not to argue for it.

A modification of the last interpretation of paradigms should be discussed. This is the claim that there is a sense in which objectivity is itself a paradigm. Such a claim is made in the works of Michael Polanyi, who argues that opting for the scientific method involves believing that it can yield objective results and committing oneself to the rules for pursuing this aim, and that this option requires a 'leap of faith' (in Polanyi's earlier works, 'personal commitment'; in his later one, commitment to 'social values').[25]

This view may be interpreted in two ways, neither of which supports anti-objectivism. It may mean that adopting a scientific approach to the acquiring of beliefs is irrational, but this would miss the point. What is at issue is whether objectivity is possible for those who adopt this approach, not whether people are objective in their adopting or rejecting of it (though were objectivity shown to be possible, then the recognition of this fact might lead people rationally to adopt the scientific approach). It may also be that one can only believe that objectivity is possible by a leap of faith, but this amounts to agnosticism regarding the issue, which is tantamount to anti-objectivism, and hence cannot be an argument for anti-objectivism but requires support. Indeed the support Polanyi does offer is mainly historical.

THE HISTORY OF SCIENCE

The paradigm-type analysis of scientific theories is, as has been noted, closely related to an appeal by anti-objectivists to the history of science. Kuhn and Feyerabend both think that the history of science illustrates and supports their view, and historians of science, like E.A. Burtt, Herbert Butterfield, and Michael Polanyi, look to the history of science to show, among other things, that scientific change is not prompted by the failure of some theories to describe and explain things relative to other theories, but rather by radical, extra-scientific shifts in perspective or world view on the part of scientists:

No process yet disclosed by the historical study of scientific development at all resembles the methodological stereotype of falsification by direct comparison with nature.   KUHN[26]

... we shall find that in both celestial and terrestrial physics ... change is brought about, not by new observations or additional evidence in the first instance, but by transpositions that were taking place inside the minds of the scientists themselves.   BUTTERFIELD[27]

It should be noted that, even if anti-objectivist historians were right, their theory-ladenness of facts view would not be proven. It would only be proven that, whatever promotes scientific change, it is not the failure of some theories to account for independently determinable facts. Also Kuhn's characterization of the 'stereotype' is surely too strong. Given the complexities and generality of scientific explanation, an objectivist would also want to reject this stereotype. His position need only require that observation of facts determinable independently of any particular theory which is designed to explain them can make this theory more or less probable. On the other hand, the correctness of anti-objectivist histories of scientific change could count as not unimportant evidence for the theory-ladenness view in that this view might be said best to explain why scientific changes come about in the way historians like Kuhn sketch. At any rate anti-objectivists put much stock in this historical argument.

Self-defeat

Before examining the anti-objectivists' historical claims we should look at two objections which are often raised to preclude the necessity of meeting anti-objectivism on historical grounds. One objection is that this kind of defence of anti-objectivism is most blatantly self-defeating, since the anti-objectivist is trying to base his theory of the non-objectivity of scientific inquiry on a scientific inquiry, namely the history of science.[28] Now for the reasons mentioned in chapter 1 I think that the problem of meeting the charge that his position is self-defeating is a serious one for the anti-objectivist, and this problem manifests itself in all his defences of his position, including this historical one. But there is no reason why the historical defence should be more self-defeating than any other.

It need not be the anti-objectivist's historical theory which determines the nature of the historical facts he examines (the ways scientists change their views). It may be some other theory – for instance, about the nature of human activity in general – which determines these facts and therefore indirectly the historical theory which explains them. Thus the anti-objectivist can argue that both he and an opponent share at least some theories (or paradigms, etc.), and this makes possible limited 'objective' comparison of historical facts. This path is open to Polanyi when he talks of the general moral code of 'scientific conscience' (including, no doubt, that of historical inquiry);[29] and Kuhn, in a passage in which he raises and dismisses, almost without argument, the self-defeating charge, suggests that it is not his historical theory but rather general epistemological ones which shape his conclusions.[30]

This requires either that the anti-objectivist produce some argument to show that his most general theory is not subject to the same anti-objectivist arguments as other theories or at least that he establish a hierarchy of theories such that he and an opponent could agree at some levels if not at all levels. We have seen the problems confronting the anti-objectivist in either task, but these are problems he must face regardless of whether or not he invokes historical considerations to support his position.

Justification and discovery

A second objection, elaborated by Scheffler and others,[31] invokes Hans Reichenbach's distinction between the 'context of discovery' and the 'context of justification' (sometimes also called the 'logics' of discovery and justification, or, for those who are wary of the inductivism associated with the phrase 'logic of discovery,' the 'psychology' and the 'logic' of scientific explanation). The argument in its strongest form is that historical considerations, considerations of how scientists actually come to offer the explanations they do, are irrelevant to such problems as the possibility of objectivity, because these problems have to do with the logical structure of explanation and verification, not with its psychological origins.[32] Thus whether one comes to adopt a theory by regarding facts or by regarding his navel is irrelevant to the objective truth or falsity of the theory adopted.

I shall maintain that, while there is a distinction between discovery and justification and this distinction is damaging to the anti-objectivist's historical arguments, these arguments should still be met. But first two inadequate criticisms of the objectivist use of the distinction should be examined.

One is Michael Polanyi's view of the role of 'scientific passion.' Having cited Kepler's report of the feeling of elation he experienced upon discovering the third law of motion, Polanyi claims that such emotion shows that psychological considerations have a place equally in understanding 'the course of discovery' and ' the outcome of discovery.' But as Polanyi develops his point, it seems that the 'logical function' which these passions play in his explanation are just to select those 'demonstrable facts which are of scientific interest' and to help suggest hypotheses.[33] This criticism of the discovery-justification distinction is all too typical of many criticisms. Its failing is that it merely asserts what the adherents of the distinction are concerned to deny – that there *is* no clear distinction. All that is offered in support is that in selecting facts to explain and in inventing hypotheses scientists are sometimes guided by extra-rational considerations. But even the most determined adherent of the distinction in question can admit this and still hold the distinction.

Another criticism of the discovery-justification distinction is found, at least in germ, in a paper by Michael Scriven.[34] Unlike most criticisms of the distinction, this one argues for abandoning it by appealing to the nature of scientific explanation. Scriven tries to show that 'understanding,' a part of the psychology of scientific inquiry, is 'logical ... , justificatory, and an essential part of the reconstruction of science and not just of its construction.' The ground for this assertion is that the test for a person's having understanding (or insight, 'instant understanding') is exactly the same as that for his having at hand a corresponding explanation, specifically whether he can fit the *explanandum* into a 'pattern' in such a way as to 'generate new truths.' This argument is advanced by Scriven as resting on the view, opposed to that of Hempel and other defenders of the deductive-nomological model, that explanation is 'reduction to the comprehensible' or fitting into a 'pattern.' But the discovery-justification distinction is still maintained, since how one comes to fit some *explanandum* into a pattern (what originally inspires him to think of the pattern) and the fitting or not fitting of it into the pattern (the scientists ability or lack of it to generate truths while thinking in terms of the pattern) are still two different matters.

Failure of criticisms of the discovery-justification distinction point up the fact that there is an important difference between the origin and the justification of scientific views, and surely deciding on the possibility of objectivity has to do with the latter. But still I do not think that the objectivist should invoke this distinction to dismiss all anti-objectivist historical arguments. The anti-objectivist's historical argument is not just that the hypotheses of a science (or at least very basic hypotheses) are arrived at extra-objectively, but that they are also accepted and sustained in such ways. And surely the objectivist wants to hold that recognition of the objective truth of some conclusion (or of something dependent on it) can be one of the causes for accepting or at least sustaining a scientific belief.[35] Otherwise the possibility of objectivity for which he argues would remain only that; his argument would only support a utopian ideal. Moreover, the objectivist's views of the structure of scientific justification are often based on or illustrated by historical surveys of the development of science, which no doubt includes or assumes elementary laws of the sociology of knowledge, and surely the objectivist would not want to deny that his belief in *these* laws is objectively sustained.

Progress and revolution in science

Fortunately the discovery-justification distinction is not needed to criticize the anti-objectivists historical arguments. On the face of it such arguments seem to be blatantly wrong. The whole history of science seems to speak against them. Why, if the anti-objectivist historians are correct, have scientists pursued experimentation and observation with such rigour? Why the elaborate experimental and statistical devices for accurate measurement and control? Why have major turning points in the history of science *followed* observations like those of Tycho Brahe and experiments like that of Michelson and Morley (both cases, interestingly, in which the experimenters held theories not supported by their observations)? Indeed anti-objectivists do not usually attempt to prove their case by direct reference to specific historical events; or rather, when they do make such an attempt, it is either in contradiction with fact or does not prove what it purports to prove.

For example, Butterfield begins *The Origin of Modern Science* with a chapter called 'The Historical Importance of Impetus' in which he portrays the abandonment of the Aristotelian theory of one kind of motion (that a moving object keeps pulling air from in front of it which then creates a wind from behind) as a paradigm of extra-objective scientific change:

We have to recognise that here was a problem of a fundamental nature, and it could not be solved by close observation within the framework of the older system of ideas ... [36]

However observations within the older 'framework' (that tops move in one place and flat-backed projectiles move as rapidly as ones with pointed backs) could and did have an effect on the abandonment of this Aristotelian theory, as we are told by objectivist historians of science like Stephen Mason,[37] and later on in his book by Butterfield himself![38]

Polanyi's works abound with reference to occurrences in the history of science which, though interesting, fail to support the anti-objectivist position. He notes many cases of observations of recalcitrant facts being explained away, of errors in measurement, and of false interpretations of observations. But such examples in no way prove, as Polanyi implies they are suppose to, that scientists do not change or sustain their views in accord with observations; they only prove that the observations are sometimes inaccurately made or falsely interpreted. In fact, Polanyi himself sometimes admits in his exposition of the examples that it is by further *observation* that the inaccuracies and falsities are discovered.[39]

Possibly in the light of the *prima facie* lack of support of their position given by the history of science, most anti-objectivists appeal not directly to particular facts but rather to interpretations of the whole history of science. A general overview of this history is said to reveal not a steady progress of alternating observation and explanation, but rather short periods of radical transformation with long periods of working out the details in between (most often mentioned are the transitions from Aristotelian to Galilean theories and from Newtonian to Einsteinian ones). It is further noted that in the fallow years observations which do not fit the last major theoretical changes are overlooked or falsely interpreted and that the theories which initiate radical change often precede experimentation. This presumably shows how initiators of change are 'set' to change, and after changes scientists are 'set' to maintain the new theories, in both cases regardless of observational evidence or counterevidence. The whole process is compared by Kuhn and others to a history of political revolutions – violent and radical changes separated by periods of social rest.

In the first place this overall picture is hard to maintain in the way anti-objectivists want. I think this is partly because, while it may be that something like scientific revolutions, radical changes of perspective, exist, it seems harder to show that there is the other half, the fallow period of detail work which supports only the preceding revolution. A picture could be drawn of how at one and the same time both the theoretical and observational work done within a theory lay the ground for the abandonment of that theory (e.g., by the development of new theoretical concepts and by the quantity and scope of experimental work). In fact in their attempts to show that new theories are rooted in other theoretical thought (as opposed to reflection on observations) anti-objectivist historians sometimes suggest evolutionary pictures of the development of scientific theories which would tend to refute their insistence on a revolutionary model. For instance, Butterfield sees the impetus theory as a transition to the inertial one, Kuhn sees the phlogiston theory as a transition to the oxygen theory, and Burtt and Butterfield see Gilbert's theory of universal magnetism as a transition to the theory of gravity.[40]

A more damaging criticism is that, even if this revolution interpretation of the history of science were correct, it would still not support the anti-objectivist's contention. Whether the formulation of scientific theories precedes or follows observations which corroborate them is just that kind of matter of discovery which critics of the historically based arguments are justified in deeming irrelevant, since it does not affect the acceptance of and continued adherence to the theories in question. Also to support objectivism it is enough that obervations prompt and sustain acceptance or rejection of a theory at some time, and the anti-objectivist historians admit that at least in periods of change the erstwhile ignored or misinterpreted observations play a central role.

Perhaps the interpretation under examination is supposed to gain its force from its analogy with the history of social-political revolutions. This, at any rate, is the analogy pursued throughout his book by Kuhn. Like political revolutions, scientific ones are 1 / unlikely unless there is an alternative available, 2 / not gradual but sudden, and 3 / not just of some parts of a theory, but of all of them. Perhaps the point of this analogy is to press it just one step further and argue 4 / that just as political revolutions are supposedly non-rational (i.e., there is nothing corresponding to objectivity in them and they involve high emotion), so are scientific ones.[41] However, even if it were the case (which I believe it is not) that social and political revolutions could not be rational, extending the analogy would itself need to be defended.

Anti-objectivist historical arguments seem to depend for much of their force on a certain image of what the history of science would have to be if objectivism were correct. In terms of this image scientific inquiry would be a sort of uninterrupted and evenly accelerating series of hypotheses and observations. But objectivism does not require that the history of science progress in this way. Facing, as he does, subject-matters of varying degrees and kinds of complexity, having at his disposal various kinds of facilities and tools not always adequate for his needs, and responding in part to different and changing social requirements, the scientist cannot be expected to pursue his work in such a linear fashion. Moreover the objectivist need not hold that observation and deduction are the scientist's only tools. Considerations of simplicity, for example, are also important parts of his arsenal.

Two passages from one of Polanyi's works will illustrate the anti-objectivist's oversimplification of what objectivism entails:

The part played by new observations and experiment in the process of discovery in science is usually over-estimated. The popular conception of the scientist patiently collecting observations, unprejudiced by any theory, until finally he succeeds in establishing a great new generalization is quite false.

We may conclude that just as there is no proof of a proposition in natural science which cannot conceivably turn out to be incomplete, so also there is no refutation which cannot conceivably turn out to have been unfounded. There is a residue of personal judgement required in deciding ... what weight to attach to any particular set of evidence in regard to the validity of a particular proposition.[42]

Polanyi thinks the view of science pictured in the first passage is wrong because scientists often invent theories before observations which verify them; and the conclusion of the second passage attacks the same concept of science and is based on the fact that scientists will often refuse to give up a theory when confronted by counter-examples. It is the view that an objective science, if there could be one, would be as described in the first passage, that I think underlies the interpretations of the history of science which the anti-objectivist offers as a criticism of objectivism.

There is a view of the nature of scientific inquiry, quite well established in the philosophy of science, which can account for the kinds of facts often appealed to by anti-objectivists but without supporting their conclusions. This alternate view hinges on a distinction between theories (theoretical laws plus definitions and categorizations) and observational laws. As Wilfrid Sellars points out, theories do not explain particular observable events by making law-like statements directly about them; this is done rather by appealing to observation laws: theories explain 'why observation laws hold.'[43] Given observation laws of, e.g., regularities in the observed relative positions of the planets or the relations in a gas between temperature and volume, theories are put forth to explain why these regularities obtain, e.g., the heliocentric theory of the solar system or the molecular theory of gases.

From this distinction three consequences follow which allow for an interpretation of some of the historical features of scientific inquiry which is compatible with objectivism. One consequence is that theories are not *directly* testable; they are testable only to the extent that laws which they purport to explain tend to hold. There is bound to be a gap between theories and observation laws, owing to the generality and scope of the former. Only in a closed system of few variables could perfect theoretical knowledge be attained, and it so happens that, except in artificially produced cases, the nature of scientific subject-matters just does not permit of perfect knowledge. But far from it being the case, as Feyerabend and others seem to suggest, that this makes objective knowledge impossible, it is often only by means of very general theories that the welter of observational data can be organized in order to discover (objectively) true laws.

A second consequence is that alternate candidates for explaining observation laws will usually be available. Not being directly testable, explanations of the observed regularities can only be limited (at least initially, before there are other, well confirmed theories to serve as limits) by the imagination of the scientist. A third consequence is that not all scientific work will involve observation; some purely theoretical work will be required – sharpening definitions, tracing internal logical relations within a theory, relating one theory to others, typological work, etc. Indeed a very few observations may spark considerable theoretical work.

The implications of these consequences for the anti-objectivist interpretation of the history of science should be clear. One way of testing a theory so as to decide among rival ones is by working within the structure of the theory to predict new observation laws. Hence it is to be expected that theoretical work will often precede observation and that statements of the hypothesized observations will be couched in the language of the theory. Since alternate theories may account for the same laws, more than just accord with observational fact will be of concern in the evaluation of theories (e.g., there will be appeal to simplicity and accord with the theories of related fields of inquiry). Since some important scientific work is intra-theoretical, some scientists can be expected to show a lack of concern with experimental work, and this is justified, because theoretical work is needed to expand the scope of theories and to relate them to other theories the better to discover truths about their subject-matters. Similarly, to the extent that a theory has succeeded in explaining and relating several different kinds of obervation laws, has achieved internal consistency and simplicity, is supported by other theories, etc., a scientist would be not only psychologically ill-disposed but also unjustified in abandoning the theory because it fails to account for some one observation law, but he would be justified in (and disposed to) looking first to the possibility of minor adjustments in the theory.

Any interpretation of the relation between theories and observations faces difficult philosophical problems, like accounting for the shiftability of the line between theoretical and observation terms and deciding the status of theoretical entities. But these are problems faced by all philosophers of science, and, in any case, the kind of interpretation of the enterprise of scientific inquiry open to the objectivist is one which allows him to accept many of the anti-objectivist historian's claims, without drawing the drastic conclusions of anti-objectivism. To disallow an objectivist interpretation of the general history of science anti-objectivist would have to clarify their own interpretations and produce much more detailed defences of them. Perhaps one reason that anti-objectivists do not seem concerned to do this is that they believe the objectivist position is seriously weakened independently by conclusions of work in the philosophies of language and perception, to which work all the anti-objectivists so far discussed frequently refer.

CHAPTER THREE Linguistic relativism

Anti-objectivist social theorists often appeal to the work of linguists and philosophers of language for support of their positions. One such theorist, Aaron Cicourel, even claims to rest his entire case on this support:

My basic assumption is that the clarification of sociological language is important because linguistic structure and use affect the way people interpret and describe the world.[1]

In fact Cicourel has more kinds of defences of anti-objectivism in the social sciences, but, like other anti-objectivists, he does indeed frequently rely on the position often called 'linguistic relativism.' And, also like other anti-objectivists, in lieu of independent defence of this position, he cites its two most famous defenders in North America, Benjamin Lee Whorf and Eduard Sapir.

OBJECTIVISM AND LANGUAGE

The position of these linguists is roughly expressed by them thus:[2]

We are ... introduced to a new principle of relativity, which holds that all observers are not led by the same physical evidence to the same picture of the universe, unless their linguistic backgrounds are similar, or can in some way be calibrated. WHORF

The fact of the matter is that the 'real world' is to a large extent unconsciously built up on the language habits of the group. No two languages are ever sufficiently similar to be considered as representing the same social reality. The worlds in which different societies live are distinct worlds, not merely the same world with different labels attached. SAPIR

The thesis is by no means unique to these men, but has a history which includes linguists of the Humboldtian tradition and philosophers like Cassirer.[3] However it is to Whorf and Sapir that many English speaking theorists harken, and (although Whorf was not careful or systematic in his elaborations of linguistic relativism, as his many critics point out) it is in Whorf's works especially that the thesis is most broadly defended, for the seeds of almost all the kinds of defence of it are to be found there.

In its full-blown form the Whorf-Sapir thesis is that how the world is perceived depends upon one's 'thought world' (also called his 'metaphysics' or 'world view'), which thought world is either wholly determined by the language he uses (especially by the grammar) or, Whorf being unclear on this point, is dialectically related to language, but language is dominant. Both the thought world and its relation to language are 'hidden' from us, but nonetheless they unconsciously cause us to categorize, describe, and interpret the world and also to behave non-verbally in certain ways.[4]

Even as summarized this account of the thesis is vague, and I think it can be shown that making the thesis more precise is costly to its basic thrust. But its implication for the objectivism – anti-objectivism debate is clear enough. The anti-objectivist wants to hold that somewhere in the machinery of description and explanation the nature of what one *can* describe and explain is determined. Linguistic relativism would assure this insofar as all social (and extra-social) inquirers grow up with certain languages and use certain languages in their inquiries. Their languages would determine what they can experience; so objective debate between two scientists with sufficiently different linguistic backgrounds would be impossible.

Before looking at Whorf's and others' arguments for linguistic relativism it will be instructive to mention three other theses which, though separate from linguistic relativism, are intermingled with it by Whorf in his account of linguistic relativism. Part of the plausibility some social theorists have seen in linguistic relativism may be due to their confusion of it with one of these other positions.

There is to be found in the work of Whorf and Sapir a thesis weaker than linguistic relativism which may be called linguistic determinism:[5]

... the 'linguistic relativity principle' ... means, in informal terms, that users of markedly different grammars are pointed by their grammars toward different types of observations and different evaluations of externally similar acts of observation, and hence are not equivalent as observers but must arrive at somewhat different views of the world.   WHORF

Language is not merely a more or less systematic inventory of the various items of experience which seem relevant to the individual ... but is also a self-contained, creative symbolic organization, which not only refers to experience largely acquired without its help but actually defines experience for us by reason of its formal completeness and because of our unconscious projection of its implicit expectations into the field of experience.   SAPIR

Now the conclusion of Whorf's argument here might be that of linguistic relativism, but the premise does not support that view. It states only that the terms and grammar we use point us toward different types of things. And one of the reasons for linguistic permeation of our experience for Sapir is the 'projection' of 'implicit expectations' by our language. Neither of these arguments alone supports the view that speakers of different kinds of languages cannot share a common experience; they assert only that the language a person uses disposes him to notice different aspects of his environment. To be sure there is experimental evidence that, for example, knowing the word for a certain kind of object facilitates one's recognitions of its tokens,[6] but Whorf, Sapir, and other linguistic relativists do not offer evidence that it is psychologically impossible for users of even very different languages to recognize the same aspects of an environment, even though a speaker of one language may more readily recognize certain of these aspects.

Nevertheless the possibility of empirical support for linguistic determinism seems remote, especially since mere correlation of terms for certain kinds of objects on the one hand and felicitous recognition of those objects on the other are more plausibly explained by the theory that both are determined by one's needs and beliefs rather than that the latter is determined by the former.[7] But even if linguistic determinism were true for large classes of behaviour, it is still not identical with the much more radical thesis of linguistic relativism, and from the point of view of arguments for anti-objectivism it is this latter thesis which is required.

Another view not clearly distinguished from linguistic relativism by Whorf and others is the methodological one that studying the grammar of languages used in different cultures is a valuable tool for the ethnologist in his studies of those cultures. For example, Whorf notes that in studying Hopi religion one would be aided by a careful study of Hopi grammar, which reveals that the Hopi word for 'cloud' is in a category reserved for reference to animate objects. And one of the motivations of Sapir's work was to promote interdisciplinary cooperation between anthropologists and linguists.[8]

If linguistic relativism were true, it would be advisable to study a language in order to study the beliefs of its users (although, of course, if linguistic relativism were true, this study would itself be shaped by the effects of the ethnologist's language on him). However it does seem that it would also be advisable to pursue the union of linguistics with other social-scientific fields even if linguistic relativism were false, since the grammar and vocabulary of different peoples might offer clues to their beliefs. The point is that the plausibility of methodological claims like Sapir's should not confer plausibility upon the claims of linguistic relativism.

A third thesis, so remote from linguistic relativism as to be inconsistent with it, is the view that some languages mask reality, while others do not. This view is especially strong in what critics of Whorf have noted, correctly I think, as his Bergsonian sympathies.[9] It is the view that primitive man, being unclouded by the artificial and abstract concepts of modern science and philosophy, has a special insight into the nature of things, and that by studying his language (or myths, rituals, etc.) we can share in his insights. Whorf maintains that the thought world of noun-dominated languages of 'standard European peoples' emphasizes 'things,' while that of the Hopi Indian, with his verb-dominated language, emphasizes 'events (or better ''eventings'')' and 'duration.'[10] Whorf makes it clear that he thinks the Hopi view is (objectively) closer to the truth:

Instead of our linguistically promoted objectification of that datum of consciousness we call 'time,' the Hopi language has not laid down any pattern that would cloak the subjective 'becoming later' that is the essence of time.[11]

Clearly if Whorf thinks that some languages inhibit while others do not inhibit gaining true beliefs about the world and that it is possible to escape the bounds of the inhibiting ones (in Whorf's case by learning the Hopi language), then even if his argument were sound he would assume the objectivist position. Again, to someone convinced by the speculative anthropology of men like Mircea Eliade or Paul Radin,[12] this view would be a plausible one, but this plausibility cannot be consistently carried to linguistic relativism.

EMPIRICAL ARGUMENTS

Most of Whorf's defences of linguistic relativism are empirical. He seeks to find significant correlations between certain kinds of languages and kinds of (non-linguistic) behaviour, and between certain kinds of languages and kinds of 'thought worlds.' He also cites empirical problems in translation. In addition Whorf presents what is best considered a non-empirical argument that, primarily due to our need to categorize, a language must 'embody' a metaphysics. While these kinds of arguments are intermingled in the presentations of most linguistic relativists, they might profitably be considered separately here in order to indicate the very serious problems attaching to each view, at least as they are employed in defence of anti-objectivism.

Language and belief

One set of Whorf's examples of the linguistic determination of non-linguistic behaviour seems to me symptomatic of all such defenses. He lists some not too common instances of fire-causing activity, e.g., smoking around empty gas drums and overheating insulation made of limestone in a distillation plant. These activities, he claims, were caused by people's being misled by the words 'empty' and 'stone,' with their connotations of 'safe' and 'fireproof,' into being careless in the circumstances described.[13] Assuming that these were not isolated cases, Whorf has here some correlation between the way speakers of the English language would describe a situation and the way they would tend to act in that situation. The problem for Whorf is in explaining this correlation in a way which would support linguistic relativism. But, no matter how words connote one another, such correlations do not seem to support this thesis.

If 'safe' is part of the meaning of 'empty,' then the fact that people act as if something they describe as empty is also safe just reveals the unsurprising fact that in using their language they correctly report their (perhaps mistaken) beliefs. If, as Whorf is more inclined to think, 'safe' is not included in the meaning of 'empty,' but is just associated with it – since most cases of something being empty are cases of its being safe – then again failure to act cautiously around things described as empty is not surprising. In both cases the correlation, though it *might* be explicable by reference to the theory of linguistic relativism, is more simply explained just by reference to one's beliefs and their effects on both his linguistic and non-linguistic behaviour. The point of focusing on this rather transparently inconclusive argument is that other arguments from the correlation of language and behaviour seem finally to be on a par with it. A correlation, if indeed it obtains, between certain examples of language usage and certain kinds of behaviour does not by itself provide evidence for linguistic relativism, but can be explained more simply by reference to the beliefs (desires, etc.) of the language users.

Into this class of arguments are to be placed the belaboured examples of Eskimos having many words for snow and the inhabitants of some tropical islands having many words for palm trees; given their experiences with and interest in these kinds of objects, why shouldn't they?[14] To take a more developed and popular argument of Whorf, he argues that there is a correlation between certain characteristics of Hopi time-expressions and their behaviour. While we use nouns to express durations, like days or seasons, the Hopi use 'a kind of adverb'; we have tenses of verbs referring to an absolute past and a future (so Whorf claims), but the Hopi verb tenses refer to a speaker's memories and anticipations, and so on. These linguistic features are correlated with characteristically Hopi 'preparing' behaviour:

Our behaviour, and that of Hopi, can be seen to be coordinated in many ways to the linguistically conditioned microcosm. As in my fire casebook, people act about situations in ways which are like the ways they talk about them. A characteristic of Hopi behavior is the emphasis on preparation.[15]

Assuming that Whorf has correctly interpreted the 'references' of English and Hopi verb tenses and assuming there is a correlation between use of these verb forms and some kind of preparing behaviour, the correlation can, again, be explained by reference to the beliefs, needs, etc., of the Hopi. For example, lacking complicated technology, social and legal organizations, and so on, their thoughts concerning the future may be restricted to plans about the immediate future, and there may be too little incentive and knowledge for them to develop linguistic means of marking off longer and more regular time sequences.

However another problem with Whorf's example is that the correlation itself seems strained. Do not *all* people prepare in just the way he says the Hopi do? Perhaps the Hopi prepare *only* in this way, not also preparing for the next year or decade, but this would be easily explained in the way suggested above. Whorf himself seems aware of this problem, since he later elaborates on the nature of the effects of Hopi language:

This is the way the Hopi deal with the future – by working within a present situation which is expected to carry impresses, both obvious and occult, forward into the future event of interest. One might say that Hopi society understands our proverb 'Well begun is half done,' but not our 'Tomorrow is another day.'[16]

Here Whorf includes not just overt behaviour but also expectations and Hopi understanding; that is, he now correlates language not just with behaviour but also with some beliefs. The suggestion is that it is certain very general attitudes toward the world that determine behaviour, but that these attitudes are themselves caused by the language of those who hold them.

Whorf pursues this view throughout his uncovering of a Bergsonian thought world in Hopi. The use of verbs and adverbs in place of what in English would be nouns, the division of tenses in terms of the relation of the speaker to his expectations and memories, the absence of forms for expressing time units cardinally, all these point to a thought world populated by events of certain durations measured by the efforts, memories, and anticipations of agents who speak the language.

A causal correlation like this might be thought to circumvent the earlier objection, since, if it held, both behaviour and underlying beliefs would depend on language; however Whorf confronts a more difficult problem here in the verification of the asserted correlation. The problem comes with Whorf's definition of 'thought world.' In a typical passage he defines it:

By 'habitual thought' and 'thought world' I mean more than simply language, i.e., than the linguistic patterns themselves. I include all the analogical and suggestive value of the patterns (e.g., our 'imaginary space' and its distant implications), and all the give and take between language and the culture as a whole, wherein is a vast amount that is not linguistic but yet shows the shaping influence of language. In brief, this 'thought world' is the microcosm that each man carries about within himself, by which he measures and understands what he can of the macrocosm.[17]

The puzzling phrase here is 'more than simply language.' Apparently Whorf means to say that part of one's thought world is language and part something else – perhaps basic (common sense) theories about the nature of space, for instance. Hence the thought world seems to split into a linguistic and an extra-linguistic element.

Cryptotypes

In other places, when Whorf talks of 'cryptotypes,' he is even less clear:

From phenomena [like the fact that phrases starting with the English 'begins' are sometimes translated by the Hopi analogue of the future tense, sometimes not] which ... pervade all Hopi grammar, I conclude that there must be to the Hopi speaker a dimly felt relation of similarity between the verb usages in each group having to do with some inobvious facet of their meaning, and therefore itself a meaning, but one so nearly at or below the threshold of conscious thinking that it cannot be put into words by the user and eludes translation. To isolate, characterize, and understand the operation of these dimly felt, barely conscious (or even unconscious) meanings is the object of my further analysis. Such an elusive, hidden, but functionally important meaning I call a CRYPTOTYPE.[18]

Here a cryptotype seems to be a meaning and a part of language which, though affecting thought, is not itself usually recognized or expressed. It is also unclear in Whorf what the relation between thought worlds and cryptotypes is – are they the same thing or is the latter a cause of the former? The unclear status and nature of thought worlds have not gone unnoticed by Whorf's critics, many of whom see the danger of tautology in this defence of linguistic relativism. To avert this danger a linguistic relativist would, unlike Whorf (so his critics argue),[19] have to find independent means of identifying a person's thought world and those aspects of his language – like his 'basic linguistic patterns' – which are causally connected with this thought world.

As Milton Singer, defending Whorf, has pointed out, circular reasoning *need* not be a problem for the linguistic relativist, but the fact that Whorf's position does seem to lend itself to this criticism is instructive. In a symposium on the Whorf-Sapir hypothesis Singer defends the hypothesis against tautology and says:

... if you have the statement, which you might call a 'linguistic proposition,' about a language, that certain categories are dominant in this language ... that is the premise. The conclusion of inference [non-circularly] drawn from that might be, right or wrong, that users of that language habitually are led to perceive or think about a certain area of experience that is related to this category.[20]

In order for there not to be circular reasoning here it must be possible to identify the way the language users perceive or think about some matter independently of the purported linguistic causes of that perception and thought.

Singer points out that this can be done by reference to 'non-verbal behaviour' and to verbal behaviour which is not the same verbal behaviour involved in the causes of the thinking and perceiving. However Singer's inclusion of verbal evidence of one's way of thinking and perceiving indicates that he has too narrow a view of the correlation between language and thought. He seems to think of it as a correspondence between some easily identifiable characteristics of language (e.g., a preponderance of verbs) and corresponding characteristics of thought (e.g., attaching importance to time). Even apart from the problem of showing what kinds of (verbal or non-verbal) behaviour could indicate 'attaching importance to time' (Singer's phrase), a positive correlation between having many verbs and having this attitude seems too weak for linguistic relativism. More would be needed to demonstrate a direct causal correlation as well as its direction.

The same problem which the Whorf hypothesis faced in the case of linguistic and extra-linguistic behaviour seems to recur here. Even if correlations of specific and easily identifiable linguistic phenomena with attitudes, beliefs, needs, etc., can be found, the correlation is not most plausibly explained by reference to linguistic relativism. It is for this reason that I think Whorf introduced, from the side of language, cryptotypes and, from the side of thought, thought worlds (giving Whorf the benefit of assuming they are different for him).

Cryptotypes and thought worlds are theoretically hypothesized entities – the one a hidden grammar, the other, not just one's beliefs, but his most basic beliefs, organized into an unconscious theory of life. These are the vital links in the causal chain which make linguistic relativism at least plausible. However if cryptotypes and thought worlds are theoretical entities, then this kind of empirical support for linguistic relativism seems far too weak. If there *is* a correlation between overt linguistic behaviour and everyday beliefs (over and above the use of the former to express the latter), then the cryptotype – thought world theory is just one way of explaining this with nothing special to recommend it, given the unclear explication of these two concepts. To the extent that it is doubtful that there *are* such correlations, the introduction of cryptotypes and thought worlds takes on a hypothesis-saving aspect – hence the suspicion of Whorf's critics that there is something tautological or question-begging about his treatment of them.

This problem is endemic to empirical arguments for linguistic relativism. If appeal is made to overt linguistic behaviour and extra-linguistic behaviour or everyday beliefs, there seems to be insufficient evidence for the thesis; if appeal is made to hidden grammars and thought worlds, then linguistic relativism is just one theory among others, and not a very plausible one. Examples of this problem can be seen in different attempts to spell out ways of testing the hypothesis. For instance, Abraham Kaplan holds that the thesis can be tested by employing 'characterology' on a societal scale by dividing societies into 'traits,' one of which is language, and then showing that, whatever the causes, from some kinds of traits in a society the nature of other traits can be inferred,[21] but this approach could at best discover correlations susceptible of many explanations.

Again, in one of the few attempts to give clear meaning to Whorfian 'cryptotypes,' Stephen Ullman compares different languages according to the proportion of words which are highly 'motivated,' 'generic,' 'polysemous,' etc.[22] But when he suggests that these classifications can help to test the Whorf-Sapir hypothesis, it is hard to see how anything as strong as linguistic relativism could be supported. The only useful suggestions of Ullman are that the preponderance of specific versus generic terms might be correlated with some kind of thought patterns and that a high proportion of 'morphologically motivated' words in German may have encouraged Martin Heidegger's penchant for etymologizing. But he does not show how having a preponderance of general or specific terms could affect thought; and the example he gives of French and German does not help, since the speakers of these two languages can exchange scientific and philosophic ideas. The Heidegger example might be shown to have some force toward strengthening the position of linguistic determinism, but, since not all German philosophers share Heidegger's penchant while some non-Germans do, it, too, seems to offer no support for linguistic relativism. Again, parts of the thesis have been clarified and tightened at the expense of its conclusion.

Intranslatability

Another attempt to defend the Whorf-Sapir hypothesis is what can be called the 'failure of translation argument.' One of Whorf's critics sees this as his main argument:

Whorf [seems to have meant] to use translation as the method of calibrating two linguistic backgrounds, [and it seems] that he identified the possibility or ease of translation with a calibrated similarity of linguistic backgrounds, and that he believed in the essential intranslatability, e.g., of Hopi, Shawnee, or Nootka into English ... [23]

It is true that, if linguistic relativism were correct, translation, except in a limited way, would be impossible, since no two languages sufficiently remote in grammar and vocabulary could express the same beliefs; but there are more causes of intranslatability than this. For instance, Harry Hoijer, usually a defender of Whorf, notes that translation may often be inhibited by absence of isomorphism of structure:

To translate from English into Navaho, or vice versa, frequently involves much circumlocution, since what is easy to express in one language, by virtue of its lexical and grammatical techniques, is often difficult to phrase in the other. A simple illustration is found when we try to translate the English phrases *his horse* and *his horses* into Navaho, which not only lacks a plural category for nouns ... but lacks as well the English distinction between *his, hers, its,* and *their* ... [24]

Hoijer goes on to note that Navaho distinctions, as between 'his' and 'hers,' depend on the context of utterance. So while a simple, non-circumlocutious translation might be impossible, linguistic relativism is not the basis of the difficulty.

Nor would linguistic relativism give the cause of intranslatability when very different sets of beliefs are being translated. For example, one defender of Whorf notes that translations of Plotinus into Latin were exceedingly clumsy, and concludes that the clumsiness 'certainly was an inhibiting factor in the spread of Neo-Platonic philosophy in that period.'[25] Aside from the fact that this example is better suited to a defence of linguistic determinism than of linguistic relativism, the conclusion is dubious.

Why not say that clumsy translations resulted from non-Plotinian beliefs? Some Greek philosophy was translated into Latin employing latinized Greek words. Why could this not also have been done with Plotinus had there been sufficient interest in and understanding of his views? To disallow accounts of intranslatability which appeal to practical problems and differences of belief, the linguistic relativist may be tempted to assert that the differences in belief and circumstance giving rise to practical problems are themselves results of linguistically determined differences in basic world views. But then he would once more be in danger of hypothesis-saving (in a pejorative sense) unless he could give some reason for adopting this view over the others.

One argument which purports to show intranslatability in principle is that of W.V.O. Quine in *Word and Object*. There, in a footnote, he makes reference to Whorf and reinterprets Whorf's thesis in the light of his theory of translational indeterminacy:

One frequently hears it urged that deep differences of language carry with them ultimate differences in the way one thinks, or looks upon the world. I would urge that what is most generally involved is indeterminacy of correlation. There is less basis of comparison – less sense in saying what is good translation and what is bad – the farther we get from sentences with visibly direct conditioning to non-verbal stimuli and the farther we get off home ground.[26]

There has been no small debate on just what Quine is up to here. If he wants to remain true to his famous attacks on the analytic-synthetic distinction, then he must support the impossibility of translation, i.e., of putting the meanings of expressions in one language into the expressions of another, not for Whorf's reasons however, but because on his account there are no such things as meanings to be translated. Quine himself ties his view of translational indeterminacy to a general theory about the empirical underdetermination of (common sense and scientific) theories, i.e., to his reflections on the consequences of the claim that it is possible for opposing theories to account equally well for all the same observations (actual or possible).[27] Such reflections, as noted in chapter 1 in connection with the arguments for anti-objectivism from selection, confront one with the danger of thoroughgoing scepticism – although, thus confronted, Quine seems to opt for objectivism (whether consistently with all his views or not).[28]

Regardless of Quine's own views, his treatment of translational indeterminacy does suggest one line of defence for the Whorf-Sapir hypothesis in that a kind of scepticism regarding translation could be generated out of it, which might be appealed to in support of anti-objectivism. Inspired by Quine, one might argue that any hypothesis of either intensional or extensional identity might be mistaken, due to very different 'conceptual schemes' of speakers, which schemes nonetheless prompt similar verbal response. Thus in his example of the English speaker and the native, Quine notes that two speakers may use 'rabbit' and 'gavagai' in all and only the same circumstances, but one mean to refer to the object, rabbit, the other to stages of a rabbit.[29]

One problem with such as argument is that it is not certain just how far this scepticism could go. As a theory regarding translation, it is discussed by Quine in connection with the remote possibilities of radical translation between users of the English language and Martians or isolated 'jungle' dwellers; and unless it were conjoined with Quine's argument about empirical underdetermination and/or his general attack on the analytic-synthetic distinction,[30] such translational indeterminacy need not be an insuperable obstacle.

In fact Quine makes use of the conclusions and methods of

physiology, cultural anthropology, and psychology. In a real situation (unlike the artificial one constructed by Quine to illustrate his particular philosophical point) why could these not be employed to determine whether the conceptual schemes of different language users were radically different without having to depend on interpretations of verbal responses, and then the resultant findings be used in settling disputes over such interpretations in especially difficult cases? For instance, physiology and learning theory might indicate ranges within which humans are likely to vary, and other psychological and sociological work could help to decide whether a certain people tended to think, for instance, in terms of 'stages' or of 'objects' in general and thereby tip the scales in the case of such indeterminacy of translation.

The factual-terminological continuum

Insofar as Quine's argument about translational indeterminacy is closely related to his thesis regarding the interdependent notions of analyticity and synonymy,[31] it suggests yet another possible support for anti-objectivism, which might be mentioned here. An anti-objectivist could maintain that, if the distinction between the analytic and the synthetic cannot be upheld, then this would, at some level of explanation and description, make disputes over factual conclusions indistinguishable from terminological disputes; because in the case of merely terminological disputes (as opposed to substantive ones) what is involved is a disagreement between two disputants over how to express the same meaning; and without a concept of synonymity there is no way of delimiting such purely terminological disputes. But, the anti-objectivist might then urge, since choice of terminology is justifiable only by reference to expediency, and rival terminological formulations could be expedient for different people confronted with all the same data, objective choice (as defined here) would be impossible.

Quine's critique of the analytic-synthetic distinction raises a host of notoriously thorny philosophical issues, and is not without its problems. However I do not think that an anti-objectivist would be well advised to turn to this thesis for support. It is hard to see how the attack on the analytic-synthetic distinction could not be a thoroughgoing one, i.e., how limits could be set in such a way as to allow for there to be a (non-pragmatic) distinction between terminologically and factually based arguments in some areas of inquiry, but not in others; since the attack is a general one on the possibility of there being any criterion of analyticity. But then *any* belief and a corresponding disbelief could, in the light of all the same evidence, be equally justified, and this position would end in a thoroughgoing scepticism (about which more will be said below).

One of Whorf's persistent themes is that Hopi language contains a metaphysics. This view has been a popular one ever since Russell and other critics of subject-predicate logic suggested that the old logic and the substance-attribute metaphysics which is said to have accompanied it were promoted by the structure of European languages. While Whorf thinks that the truth of this view is illustrated by empirical linguistics, his arguments in favour of it are not entirely empirical:

Just as it is possible to have any number of geometries other than the Euclidean which give an equally perfect account of space configurations, so it is possible to have descriptions of the universe, all equally valid, that do not contain our familiar contrasts of time and space. The relativity viewpoint of modern physics is one such view conceived in mathematical terms, and the Hopi Weltanschauung is another and quite different one, non-mathematical and linguistic. Thus, the Hopi language and culture conceals a METAPHYSICS, such as our so-called naive view of space and time does, or as the relativity theory does; yet it is a different metaphysics from either.[32]

The implication is that some very general system of symbols is necessary to organize our perceptions and beliefs about the world; and languages, being kinds of symbolic systems available to all people but varying from culture to culture, will determine different systems for different people (all 'equally valid'). Associated with this view is another that, at an unconscious level of neural connections, thought and language are linked.[33] Whorf wants to advance, I believe, the often held view that thinking must be done in a language (hence strengthening his claim that languages cause the symbolic systematizations), and he speculates that this is done at a deep and hidden level (possibly to escape the intuitive counter-examples of grasping for words or trying to put some thought into language).

The view that our language must embody a metaphysics is usually defended by appeal to linguistic categories, but before this kind of argument is looked at the *prima facie* implausibility of the general thesis should not go unmentioned. In the first place, it is noteworthy that speakers of the same language have advocated radically different metaphysical theories (e.g., Descartes and Bergson, Hegel and Schopenhauer), and in the second, speakers of radically different kinds of languages have shared similar metaphysical views. Thus the fact that speakers of Finnish and Hungarian, both non-Indo-European languages, have shared religious and philosophical views with other Europeans is generally overlooked (and to explain this by saying that they share the same culture would still leave the problem of showing how they could share the same culture if their language-caused *Weltanschauungen* made objective communication impossible).

Perhaps this theory has appealed to some because of confusion about what it is that determines a metaphysics or world view. No doubt some inference about the kind of philosophies a society is likely to have, or not have, could be made from a general examination of the mode of life, level of knowledge, etc., of its people. To take an obvious example, it is unlikely that primitive tribal peoples would espouse the philosophy of Descartes. And it is also doubtful that the vocabulary and possibly even features of the syntax of primitive languages would be readily capable of expressing this world view. Such expression, if desired by these people, would perhaps be inordinately clumsy. But neither this nor cultural limitations on thought supports linguistic relativism.

Advocates of the theory that language embodies these world views speak as if an examination of a language makes clear the world view its speakers are likely to have. But is this the case? Could not, for instance, a preponderance of verbs and descriptions of objects in terms of what effects they have at different times, such as Whorf notes in Hopi, be interpreted not as reflecting a Bergsonian, duration-based world view, but as reflecting a thoroughgoing Newtonian one. Since they see time as a constant and even flow within which all objects are contained and in causal relations with one another, the Hopi would have ways in their language of marking the fact that there are no 'objects' which do not undergo these universal temporal and causal relations, hence their use of verbs, and so on.

Again Kaplan, supporting Whorf, suggests that from a language which divides nouns into those which represent different paradigms and those which represent various deviations from each paradigm, we would be justified in inferring that its users hold to a Platonic world view.[34] But from such a language we could just as easily infer that its speakers are Heraclitians who, believing that all is in flux, feel the need for arbitrarily specifying some objects in the flux as landmarks, and then identifying other objects by their degrees of similarity to them. Also one critic of Whorf notes that a linguist can see in west semitic language 'a personal

and subjective character which imparts to the verb a temporal orienta-
tion,' the opposite of Whorf's interpretation of this language as revealing
an 'objectifying' and 'spatially oriented' metaphysics.[35]

CLASSIFICATION

One reason that I think Whorf and other linguistic relativists are not
especially troubled to pursue an empirical defence of their view is that
they put so much weight on the argument from classification. Jost Trier,
a pioneer of this view, writes:

Every language is a system of selection over and against objective reality ... [A
person's world view is a] linguistic-conceptual realization of a view of reality
proceeding from a unique but definite structuring matrix which continuously
compares and contrasts, relates and distinguishes the data of reality.[36]

And Whorf:

We dissect nature along lines laid down by our native languages. The categories
and types that we isolate from the world of phenomena we do not find there
because they stare every observer in the face; on the contrary, the world is presented in a kaleidoscopic flux of impressions which has to be organized by our
minds – and this means largely by the linguistic systems in our minds. We cut
nature up, organize it into concepts, and ascribe significances as we do, largely
because we are parties to an agreement to organize it in this way – an agreement
that holds throughout our speech community and is codified in the patterns of
our language. The agreement is, of course, an implicit and unstated one, BUT
ITS TERMS ARE ABSOLUTELY OBLIGATORY; we cannot talk at all except by sub-
scribing to the organization and classification of data which the agreement
decrees.[37]

Different metaphysics are, then, generated in different languages by
using different principles of classification, and all language involves
some element of classifying.

Examples of classifications often given are differences in the classification of colours and of kinship relations,[38] and Whorf notes that what
is grammatically classified in English as a noun, e.g., 'lightning' (and
hence, according to him, the referent is classified as an object), is classified as a verb in Hopi (so lightning is classified as an event for them).
And he says that unlike us the Shawnee would consider 'I pull the branch
aside' and 'I have an extra toe on my foot' as referring to similar circumstances.[39]

On the face of it it is not clear that the mere need to classify, and differences of classification, could support linguistic relativism. Surely speakers of Russian and English see the same colour spectrum, both we and the Hopi observe the same flash of lightning, and the Shawnee can tell the difference between pulling branches and having extra toes. This argument for linguistic relativism requires support.

Conventionality

One support invokes an appeal to the conventionality of systems of classification. This often encountered view is that language does serve to classify things, and that all classifications, being conventional, are arbitrary.

To establish a classification it is requisite to produce a principle for dividing a genus into species, and it is true that the selection of any one principle is a matter of convention. The statements of such principles are not truth-valuable, just as stipulative definitions are not truth-valuable. To this extent systems of classification (including those ingrained in our language) might be said to be arbitrary. However this element of conventionality does not by itself support a linguistic relativist view which could establish anti-objectivism.

There is at least the objectivity of the application of classificatory systems. Whether some item is to be placed in one category or another is an empirical matter which can be (objectively) rightly or wrongly carried out. And, even more, whether some subject matter falls within the genus of a classification is also an empirical matter. As Nagel has correctly pointed out regarding measurement (taking a position which is opposed to that of anti-objectivists like Cicourel who employ the conventionality argument), not only is it an empirical matter within one system of measurement what values attach to any measured specimen, but it is also an empirical matter to determine what kinds of properties are measurable.[40]

A further, and for present purposes more important, respect in which systems of classification admit of objectivity is that the adequacy of a principle of classification can itself be objectively determined, and this in two ways. First, since classification of things is usually done for a purpose, one principle of classification may be objectively better than another for serving some purpose (e.g., dividing animals according to their modes of locomotion may be superior to a biological principle for the purpose of hunting). The appearance of pragmatism here is not incompatible with objectivity, since both the fact and the explanation of the usefulness of some principle of classification for some purpose are objectively determinable. That is, whether some principle A is useful for some purpose P depends at least in part on the truth of a law to the effect that people with purpose P using principle A usually bring about P. Further, an explanation showing *why* such a law holds is also possible (involving no doubt very complicated interrelations of psychological and sociological laws and those governing the behaviour of what is classified).

Second, there are systems of classification the purport of which is to approximate 'natural types' – i.e., to group characteristics together which are supposed to be related in law-like ways (like the various symptoms of mental illness), and there are systems of classification which purport to divide the elements of some subject-matter into categories such that there are causal relations among elements of different categories (like the divisions of society into economic and superstructural factors in Marxist social theory). Both sorts of classificatory systems are capable of being objectively altered (if the characteristics are not found to be related in law-like ways and if the causal connections cannot be confirmed).[41]

Interpretation

Another argument, more directly related to linguistic relativism and sometimes used to support the argument from conventionality, relates to what might be called the interpretive function of descriptive language and greatly strengthens linguistic determinism. One expression of P.K. Feyerabend's theory-ladenness of facts view is that 'the meanings of observational terms depend on the theory on behalf of which the observations have been made.'[42] Hence to replace one theory with another is to change the meanings of the terms employed in description and experimentation:

... introducing a new theory involves changes of outlook both with respect to the observable and with respect to the unobservable features of the world, and corresponding changes in the meanings of even the most 'fundamental' terms of the language employed.[43]

The view expressed by Feyerabend here is, roughly, that to describe is to interpret. More precisely it is the view that to describe something is to classify it as a kind of thing which is susceptible only of certain sorts of explanation and further description.

The implications of this view for the linguistic relativist argument from classification are obvious. To classify something in a certain way is not just to dispose one to think of it as the kind of thing to which only certain descriptive language is appropriate, but it is to make it impossible to think of it in any other way. Hence a religious believer describes Mr Jones's shooting of Mrs Jones as a sin and an atheistic judge as a crime, and by so doing they commit themselves to very different ways of thinking about Jones's deed (and maybe also about Jones), so much so that they could never agree on what Jones did.

Now it is true (as is sometimes pointed out by linguistic relativists) that a certain description of a kind of thing may become so firmly entrenched in the vocabulary of some person or group as to become a definition, i.e., the properties referred to become defining properties of the commonest expressions for what is described, and perhaps this is thought to be so widespread as to guarantee irreconcilable disagreement between those with different vocabularies. But even if it is sometimes unclear whether some former description is being used in such a way, this consideration is not strong enough to support linguistic relativism unless it can be shown that all differences (and changes) in descriptive language *must* reflect differences (or changes) in basic attitudes or general world outlooks regarding the referents of the descriptive terms. Or it would have to be shown that two people who classify something differently (by using different descriptive language) could not know that they were classifying the same thing.

It is hard to see how the anti-objectivist can make out such a case. Scheffler notes that, if this view were true, it would be impossible to learn how to use descriptive language at all.[44] And it does seem that people who classify an object differently can agree on a common description; for instance, both the religious believer and the atheist can surely agree on describing Mr Jones's act as 'causing Mrs Jones to stop breathing' or as 'shooting Mrs Jones'; although they will disagree about the causes and effects of what they are describing (but yet they may still be able to agree on what would count as a description of a sin, though one will deny that there could be anything truly answering to the description). Even Mary Hesse, a defender of 'meaning variance' in scientific theories, admits that in actual practice there probably never are cases where common descriptions cannot be found by scientists (and non-scientists) with rival theories.[45]

It does seem that such a common ground can always be found, barring such violent disagreement in belief that communication between the disagreeing interlocutors is sociologically impossible, e.g., by making it impossible for them to engage in discussion for the time necessary to come to agreement. On reflection it is hard to see what boundaries between systems there can be such as to prevent agreement. For example, an all-is-in-durational-becoming Bergsonian and an objectifying-spatially-oriented Platonist could reach common agreement on descriptions in terms of the extensions and directions of colours, even if one refused to describe anything as an object (although, again, I do not see why, just as in the case of 'sin,' the Bergsonian could not agree on what would count as an accurate description of an object).

As I see it, the burden placed on the linguistic relativist is to produce a criterion for setting boundaries on systems of classification, i.e., showing what it is about certain sets of descriptions that would prohibit users of them from coming to agreement with users of descriptions in some other set. I do not see where the linguistic relativist could find this criterion.

To use a linguistic criterion, like 'all those descriptions which are in the same family (or are of a certain type or category),' begs the question or at least sets it back a step to the need for giving independent criteria of families or types. To set the boundaries psychologically in terms of beliefs, so descriptions are sorted according to the beliefs of people using them, would make it impossible for two users of the same classification system to disagree about a certain tenet or set of tenets *within* their common classification system (and surely only the anti-objectivist resigned to complete scepticism could deny intra-classification 'objective' dispute). And finding a criterion for distinguishing between those beliefs which can and those which cannot be parts of the same classification system would be just as difficult as finding a criterion for setting boundaries on descriptive terms. A similar problem would beset a behavioural criterion, setting boundaries at those points where communication breaks down; since a breakdown in communication can be a result of disparity in belief without any suggestion of mutual incomprehension, some way of distinguishing between those kinds of communication failure and ones which mark different systems of classification would be needed.

The classificatory regress

An argument which might be thought to back up the arguments from conventionality and interpretation may be called the 'classificatory regress argument.' Anti-objectivists might point out that, even if two people could agree on some common description, this common description would still be a description, and hence perform some classifying function and suppose some principle of classification and therefore a metaphysics. Or, to put the same point another way, if there were two interlocutors x and y using classifications c^1 and c^2 which generate descriptions D^1 and D^2, and if they find some common description D^3, this description is generated by some other classification C^3; and a third speaker Z might not use C^3 but yet another classification scheme C^4 to provide descriptions in that circumstance. To reach agreement X, Y, and Z would have to find a fifth description, and so on.

Linguistic relativists usually defend this kind of argument by attacking the views that ordinary language, or a language referring to basic elements of experience or containing only 'protocol sentences,' can serve as final courts of appeal and stop any regress. But it is not necessary to enter into this debate to see the limitations of the regress argument (and in fact some objectivists share linguistic relativists' criticisms of these views[46]). An objectivist can agree that there is no *a priori* limit to the number and kinds of descriptions that can be made of the same subject-matter by maintaining that these descriptions need not be alternate, competing ones, but fuller and fuller descriptions of that subject matter, or perhaps just various true (or false) descriptions of it from many different points of view and for different purposes, each description (potentially) revealing genuine aspects of it. To support this interpretation of the succession of descriptions offered and offerable of things and events, the objectivist could point to the growth of knowledge and increasing control of nature achieved in the course of human history and to the widespread ability of people to communicate.

Against this what has the linguistic relativist to say in recommendation of his view? He might (arbitrarily) urge that these characteristics of the human community and its history are happy accidents, or he might argue that appeals to the history of knowledge, and the ability to communicate, beg the question; since what counts as knowledge (and history and communication) would, presumably, be determined by the categories we use at any one time. However the growth of knowledge in history seems continuous enough at least within the historiography of the contemporary anti-objectivist and his rival. And even though the anti-objectivist may urge that this historiography is just one possible one among others, he must still consider himself rationally bound by what is the case within it. If he denies that he is bound by the 'facts' of the system of thought within which he finds himself or which he adopts, then he would seem to be committed to thoroughgoing scepticism (of the Sextus Empiricus variety, discussed in chapter 1).

SCEPTICISM

This danger of thoroughgoing scepticism is a general one for advocates of the arguments for classification. Denying, as they must, that there is some rock-bottom classification system, how can they also deny that objectivity is possible for inquirers employing different systems of classification from among the indefinite possible systems (in the respect, relevant to this work, that objective agreement and disagreement is possible between users of different systems and that systems can be abandoned on objective grounds) *and* still avoid thoroughgoing scepticism? Perhaps a brief look at some ways that such scepticism might be thought to be avoided by the anti-objectivist is in order (brief for present purposes only; since each way is situated in a nest of philosophical problems of interest in themselves and in relation to other philosophical disputes).

Intra-classification scheme objectivity

One way might be to argue that objectivity is still possible within systems of classification (admitting that these systems may have no philosophically determinable boundaries). Thus it is urged that having come to 'think' within some system, we test hypotheses and settle disagreements with others who share the same system just as objectivists say we do; though we are blocked from such activity when confronted with hypotheses expressed by people using other systems.[47]

But suppose there are two scientists with different systems of classification, each of whom is justified according to *his* system in holding that the other has made all the same observations as he in the sense of having been exposed to all the same publicly observable conditions and having in fact observed them in some way determined by the respective systems. Further suppose that each has had no reason for favouring some hypothesis of his own about what is observed over any other on the basis of prior empirical or theoretical work within his system, and that each is incorrigibly justified in this belief, in that no matter what further tests either made he would not, in fact, be rationally warranted, according to his system, in disbelieving that he and the other scientist very probably had available and took note of all the same evidence.

Each scientist, on the basis of his observations of the subject matter, makes a report – reports A and B respectively. The question now is, could A be legitimately translated by the second scientist into his system as the negation of B? If it could not be so translated, then what other grounds for prohibiting such translation in principle could there be than that objectivity is to be preserved (i.e., objectivism would be presupposed)? If it could be so translated, given all that he knows, the scientist could not avoid scepticism; since he would believe, within his system, that on the basis of all the same evidence both his belief and the corresponding belief are justified.[48]

Kantianism and neo-Kantianism

Another way in which linguistic relativism might be thought to be saved from scepticism is by taking either the Kantian view that there is one set of universal categories making up all human systems of thought[49] or the view of historically- and anthropologically-minded neo-Kantians that there are classification systems for all those of a certain historical era or from one kind of culture. Thus all scientists, living in the culture and historical epoch of present-day industrial society, for example, would share the same system of thought. But neither version will do. A scientist, or anyone else, can imagine some extra-terrestrial but intelligent being or a people of a radically different culture who, though confronted with exactly the same evidence as himself (in the way discussed above) would be justified in holding a belief which he could be justified only in disbelieving. Imagining such a circumstance, how could be avoid either giving up the belief (*per impossibile*) that *his* beliefs are justified, or holding that in the event of a confrontation in which this imagined state of affairs took place (e.g., if he became an anthropologist-linguist) one person's belief at least would be objectively wrong?

The behavioural theory of meaning

A third means proposed by linguistic relativists for avoiding scepticism is to espouse what Feyerabend calls, misleadingly I think, the 'pragmatic theory of observation' or what might be labeled the 'behavioural' (or perhaps 'reactive') theory of meaning.[50] Linguistic relativists who stress the interpretive function of language flirt dangerously with thoroughgoing scepticism unless they can show some way that two theories (other than ones which require no observations for their substantiation, of course) can be said objectively to compete.[51] If two theories can share no observation terms (no matter how loosely observation term is defined or whether the line between observation and theoretical terms is clearly fixed), then there can be no basis for favouring one over the other except on merely pragmatic or aesthetic grounds.

The fact that practical needs and aesthetic tastes notoriously differ over time and from person to person would justify belief in any theory and one of its rivals by two people with all the same evidence (in the sense defined above) and having different tastes or needs. Since the effects on thought and action of such a position, if sincerely held, would be the same as the effects of scepticism, the position should surely be counted as a sceptical one. What difference is there between denying that belief in Newtonian physics is any more objectively justified than belief in Aristotelian, or vice versa, on the grounds that we can never tell whether any theory is any more true or false than a rival on the one hand, and urging, on the other, what comes to the same thing, that no theory can be shown to be a rival of any other?

The behavioural theory is supposed to prevent linguistic relativists from being driven to such a position by providing them with criteria for saying when various theories address the same subject-matter (though anti-objectivists often put the word 'same' in quotation marks, thus calling attention to the very problem under discussion). This theory shifts from consideration of the meanings of terms in theories to the behaviour or reactions of those who use theories. Two theorists are said to be addressing the same subject matter when, for instance, the one has dispositions to utter certain sounds or, as in Quine's view, has taking place certain retinal and other physiological reactions,[52] in the same circumstances that the other (ideally a robot for Feyerabend) has matching dispositions and/or reactions. So Feyerabend's pragmatic theory is supposed to make it possible to say that two theories 'share the same domain' without having to refer to a shared core of 'observational meaning.' He argues that the 'observation sentences' of a theory are those which are uttered (quickly) in some physical situation which normally prompts the sentence; and two theories cover the same domain when there is a regular correspondence between the utterings of their observation sentences (or between such utterings and the reactions of a pre-programmed robot).

The failure of this attempted escape from *de facto* scepticism, as some of Feyerabend's critics note, is that there is no way on this thesis of telling whether the correspondence holds. To do this allowance must be made for determining that the utterances of the two theory users (or their retinal reactions, or the robot's reactions) take place in the same circumstances, including internal psychological (physiological or mechanical) conditions as well as aspects of the external environment. But determining this would require at least some observation and inference; so the same problem would again arise for observers with different theories. And to try to stop the sceptical regress thus generated, as in the case of Quine, by advocating use of the scientific (or other belief-supporting) tools generally respected in one's age is to confront the problems involved in the first two attempts to escape scepticism.

Perception versus interpretation

A fourth way in which the linguistic relativist might try to avoid scepticism, suggested by Polanyi and drawing on the work of philosophers like

Carnap, is to hold that adherents of different language-embodied classification schemes are able to reach objective agreement in their perceptions of the world, and that it is only their general interpretations of the facts thus gained which are determined by their schemes.[53] So two scientists might have various disputes over what the relations among things are or what things exist, but one may subscribe (consciously or unconsciously) to a system of thought in which some things are interpreted (classified) as real in a materialist sense, while the other may interpret them as unreal, perhaps in a Platonic sense. Following Carnap, but reversing his emphasis, the linguistic relativist might urge that, while disputes of the second kind cannot be objectively decided (since they formulate 'external questions,' i.e., questions not about things but about general linguistic frameworks within which it is found expedient, given certain purposes, to place things), disputes of the first kind are objectively settlable (they formulate 'internal questions') even for users of different linguistic frameworks.

The appeal of such a view for avoiding scepticism might be prompted by the generality of the kinds of external questions usually adduced as not admitting of objective answer (e.g., 'do numbers, considered as universals, exist?'). Indeed it was to (dis)solve such profoundly difficult philosophical problems that Carnap himself developed the internal/external distinction. But I still do not see how this distinction could help the linguistic relativist to avoid scepticism, or at least a position so close to it as to be practically equivalent.

The problem is in setting a limit on what counts as a (non-objectively determinable) interpretation as opposed to what can be objectively determined. For instance, on this view would a prediction count as an interpretation or not? To make a prediction about something is surely to say more about that thing than just to report one's present perceptions of it, but if predictions are to be, or to include, interpretations, then two scientists could, on the basis of the very same evidence, make conflicting predictions (even of the most mundane sort) and be equally justified. Surely this would count as scepticism even if the two scientists could come to objective agreement on their present and perhaps past perceptions.

Another way that this view can lead to scepticism is illustrated in the following passage. R.L. Goodstein, commenting on the Aristotelian-Galilean controversy, writes:

It is not a fact which is under dispute but the choice of a mode of expression. We do not dispute the fact that different objects are seen to fall with the same speed; the question is whether we shall use a language which says that the sentence 'Different objects fall with the same speed' is *true* because we perceive that different objects fall with the same speed, or whether we shall say that it is *false* and the perception a delusion.[54]

Here the 'interpretation' of the Aristotelian justifies him in disbelieving just what he and the Galilean are supposed to be able to come to objective agreement about. And unless either some way of preventing such 'modes of expression' from counting as interpretations is found or it is held that the choice of such modes can be objective, then some such reinterpretation would always be possible for any perceptually gained beliefs, and once again scepticism would seem to result. Over and above reports of present and past observations, any limit on what is to count as an interpretation would seem arbitrary, and to insist on there being some limit on interpretations so as to disallow ones which would lead to scepticism would be to insist *a priori* on preserving objectivity (surely a peculiar anti-objectivist demand). If, on the other hand, choice of some modes of expression can be objective, why cannot the choice of any others likewise be objective?

There is another defence of anti-objectivism appealing to our need to classify suggested by Whorf when he mentions the 'kaleidoscopic flux of impressions which has to be organized by our minds.' This is the view that, either because of the nature of the world or of our sensory apparatus, we are confronted at some primary stage of experience with a chaos on which we must impose some kind of order. However this is a different kind of argument from those we have been considering in this section. It is, in fact, one of a group of arguments for anti-objectivism which claim to be based on the nature of perception.

CHAPTER FOUR **Perceptual relativism**

In his *Sociological Theory and Social Research* Charles Cooley wrote:

Regarding subjectivity, I may say that all knowledge is subjective in one sense: in the sense, namely, that it is mental, not the external thing, but a construct of the mind. Even the simplest perceptions of form or extent, much more the exact perceptions of science, far from being mere physical data, are the extended process of education, interpretation, and social evolution.[1]

This passage is one expression of what is often called perceptual relativism, the view that people's perceptions are influenced in such a way by their basic beliefs (or desires, *Weltanschauungen*, etc.) that it is impossible for two disputants with sufficiently different beliefs, etc., to come to objective agreement by appeal to perceptually gained information.

PERCEPTION AND OBJECTIVISM

It is important to keep this view separate (in a way not always done in anti-objectivist arguments) from two other views, neither of which the objectivist need reject. First, the objectivist need not hold that *all* disagreements are (objectively) settlable by reference to perceptual information. As noted in chapter 1, an objectivist may reject positivism and maintain that belief in the truth of some (non-analytic) propositions is objectively justified on non-empirical grounds (contrary to the opinion of most anti-objectivists, who equate positivism and objectivism).

Second, the objectivist can, and should, admit one kind of perceptual relativism which might be called 'perspectival relativism.' He should admit that the fact that two people simultaneously perceiving some object occupy different locations guarantees that their perceptions of it will differ insofar as they are literally from different points of view. But the objectivist can still hold that the various 'views' of the object thus gained are not ones which must yield irreconcilable conflict in the beliefs of the viewers, but are (potentially) compatible, even though someone with a very limited view may have a distorted 'picture' and be hesitant to argue that his view is compatible with another's. Indeed it is part of the effort of scientific method to minimize the possibilities of such distortion and to gain fuller and fuller 'pictures' of objects studied.

Perceptual relativism is appealed to for direct support of anti-objectivism by anti-objectivists arguing for the theory-ladenness of facts, such as Hanson and Feyerabend.[2] It is also appealed to by linguistic relativists in support of their view, which could in turn be appealed to by anti-objectivists; so Whorf and others suggest that perception, guided by linguistically determined beliefs, is somehow interpretive.[3] Perceptual relativism is often invoked to support anti-objectivism in the social sciences, but seldom with supporting arguments; rather, as in the case of Cooley, it is just assumed to be true and to support anti-objectivism in the social sciences (as elsewhere). An examination of the grounds on which perceptual (as distinguished from perspectival) relativism might be based seems to me to cast serious doubt on the doctrine's truth, but in addition I think the force of the anti-objectivist appeal to perceptual relativism is less strong than is often assumed.

In the first place, even if this view were correct, the support for anti-objectivism offered by it would not immediately follow. From the purported fact that differences in certain beliefs cause us to perceive things differently it would not directly follow that differences in those beliefs which go to make up scientific theories cause the scientists involved to perceive things differently. Unless it were argued that *all* differences in belief cause differences in perception, the anti-objectivist would have to find a way of determining just which kinds of beliefs are such that differences in them cause such perceptual disparity and then determine whether the theoretical (or related) beliefs of scientists are of this kind. The difficulties confronting such a task are, I think, underestimated by anti-objectivists. They would be of the kinds discussed in chapters 2 and 3 in connection with defining paradigms and locating boundaries of classificatory schemes and would of course include the omnipresent dangers for anti-objectivism of being self-defeating or of falling into thoroughgoing scepticism.

In the second place, I think that some of the force of those arguments which appeal to perceptual relativism to support the theory-ladenness view is dissolved when it is noted that there is a difference between what counts as an observation term in a scientific theory and what a scientist can observe. In an interesting article on the 'problem of theoretical terms' Peter Achinstein argues that what counts as an observation term in one science might not in another, and that even within one science or one theory what is to count as an observation term might depend on such decisions as how to regard the effects of something on a medium or measuring device (e.g., whether to count seeing traces of an electron in a cloud chamber as seeing the electron).[4] The point (though not one Achinstein is concerned to make) is that these are decisions which have to do with what meanings (often technical) the scientist gives to his terms, and no stand on what the scientist can observe need be entailed by the fact that different scientists draw the line between observational and theoretical terms differently.

Theory-ladenness arguments which involve perceptual relativism are, perhaps, also plagued by the confusion of the perceptual relativism dispute with two others. Grover Maxwell, in discussing the 'ontological status of theoretical entities,' complains that the realism-instrumentalism debate has been obscured by confusing it with the definitionism debate.[5] And it seems to me that the present dispute is separate from both of these. That is, an objectivist position opposed to perceptual relativism is compatible with the view that there are entities such as electrons and the view that these are convenient fictions, and it is also compatible with the view that all theoretical terms can in principle be defined by means of non-theoretical terms as well as the opposing view.[6]

Despite these reservations, however, the correctness of perceptual relativism would carry the anti-objectivist some way toward establishing his position and would be a not inconsiderable source of embarrassment for the objectivist. So arguments in favour of the position merit examination. Such arguments can be divided into two closely related groups depending on whether they appeal to the selectivity of perception or to some interpretive aspect of the perceptual process.

PERCEPTUAL SELECTIVITY

The appeal to the selectivity of perception, found for example in the work of Polanyi and Myrdal,[7] is made in a typical way by Henri Bergson:

The whole difficulty of the problem that occupies us [of understanding perception] comes from the fact that we imagine perception to be a kind of photographic view of things, taken from a fixed point by that special apparatus which is called an organ of perception ...

And in support of his criticism of the photographic view (based on a certain aspect of his metaphysics being developed at this point) Bergson gives this alternate account:

The reality of matter consists in the totality of its elements and of their actions of every kind. Our [perceptual] representation of matter is the measure of our possible action upon bodies; it results from the discarding of what has no interest for our needs, or more generally for our functions.[8]

Similarly Polanyi discusses the 'shaping of percepts' by means of 'selecting from the material presented.'[9]

Objectivists like Scheffler have (I think correctly) also rejected the photograph view of perception and agreed that perception is in some way selective,[10] but they have maintained that this does not support perceptual relativism. Were this the only support the perceptual relativist could offer, then he would be in a position similar to that of those linguistic relativists who appeal to what was called above 'linguistic determinism.' It may well be the case that the portion we perceive of a total possible field of vision (what we could physiologically perceive barring special circumstances) is determined in part by our experience and interests. A trained hunter can pick out animals in a forest which a novice could not pick out without help, and a hungry man may be more apt to smell food cooking than a companion indifferent to eating.[11] But what is at stake in the objectivist–anti-objectivist dispute is whether it is possible for people to come to perceptual agreement, not whether everyone always is in agreement.

The similarity of human sensory apparatus and the widespread ability of people to cooperate in tasks requiring perceptual agreement is evidence that such agreement is possible, even though, as in the case of the novice hunter and the sated companion, it may not always take place. Surely the novice could be taught to discriminate between animals and their forest environment, and the companion's attention could be called to the odour of food. Or where this could not be done, perhaps because of some deficiency in the sense organs, the use of scientific apparatus or the testimony of a third person could be employed to settle any disputes.

In the light of such considerations it seems to me that the selectivity of our perception could at most support a kind of expanded version of perspectival relativism, by adding a psychological as well as a spatio-temporal dimension. And if the mere fact of selectivity of perception does not support perceptual relativism, the anti-objectivist must buttress this line of argument. I find three such buttresses.

Perception and the unconscious

Polanyi offers one in his suggestion that the selection is not amenable to conscious control (that the control is unconscious, or, as some philosophers say, preconscious): 'We know that perception selects, shapes and assimilates clues by a process not explicity controlled by the perceiver.' But then Polanyi continues:

Since the powers of scientific discerning are of the same kind as those of perception, they too operate by selecting, shaping, and assimilating clues without focally attending to them. Thus it is ultimately left to the personal judgement of the scientist to decide what conflicting evidence invalidates a proposition, what things coming to his notice must be accepted as facts. ...[12]

First Polanyi says we have no (explicit) control over our perceptual selections; then he says we can have control. I believe this contradiction points to a central problem for this version of the argument from selection. It is no accident that it is scientific selection over which Polanyi holds that we have control. It has been one of the achievements of science to control perception, not only in making it precise and extending it by means of instruments beyond what human organs unaided could detect, but also in compelling scientists to change some perceptual habits (e.g., forcing them to discriminate between slightly different shades of colour or tones which outside the laboratory they might not discriminate). Or where such change is impossible, science has at least alerted them to this fact, that is, forced them to recognize that there may be qualities of objects not amenable to unaided inspection by human senses.

The fact that some of the determinations of our perceptual selections are unconscious will not support perceptual relativism unless it can be shown that they must be immune from conscious control in that we can never change unconscious perceptual habits or even become aware of them (and also of limits to perception) in a way which would enable us to allow for them. I doubt that there could be such an argument, especially since it would have to show that these unconscious determinations exist without thereby also making us aware of them in a way self-defeating to the argument, i.e., in a way which would enable us to allow for them.

Perception and the infinity of selections

Another support for the argument from the selectivity of perception appeals to the infinity of possible selections. Weber writes in this connection:

Now as soon as we attempt to reflect about the way in which life confronts us in immediate concrete situations, it presents an infinite multiplicity of successively and constantly emerging and disappearing events, both 'within' and 'outside' ourselves. The absolute infinitude of this multiplicity is seen to remain undiminished even when our attention is focused on a single 'object', ... as soon as we seriously attempt an exhaustive description of *all* the individual components of ... 'individual phenomena' ...[13]

If the possible selections are infinite, then, presumably, being able to select consciously would not help in arriving at objective conclusions, since a further selection is always available.

Now if 'selecting' means 'directing one's attention toward an aspect of his environment,' then this argument is just a species of the argument from selection discussed in chapter 1. Two scientists could still come to objective agreement (or disagreement) by attending to the same aspects of their environment, the fact that there are infinite other aspects being irrelevant. If, as is more likely, 'selecting' means 'conceptualizing,' i.e., categorizing something as a certain sort of thing,[14] then this argument becomes similar to the argument from classification discussed in chapter 3, with the difference that the conceptualization takes place somewhere in the process of perceiving rather than in that of describing (or perhaps that conceptualization is requisite for recognition instead of description) and can be met in the same way. If we are to reject thoroughgoing scepticism, then there is no reason why the view that perception involves conceptualization cannot be compatible with objectivity.

This, in fact, is the view that Scheffler takes. Seeing this conceptualization argument as the crucial one for perceptual relativism, Scheffler argues that in their use of 'conceptualization' perceptual relativists confuse categories and hypotheses:

Conceptualization relates both to the idea of categories for the sorting of items and to the idea of expectation, belief, or hypothesis as to how items will actually fit available categories; it links up with the notion of *category* and, also, with the quite different notion of *hypothesis*. The very same category system is, surely, compatible with alternative, and indeed conflicting hypotheses: that is, having adopted a given category system, our hypotheses as to the actual distribution of items within the several categories are not prejudged.[15]

Scheffler argues further that there is no theoretical justification for ruling out the possibility of different categorizations being linked in such a way that hypotheses expressed in different systems could be objectively compared.[16] There being infinite possible conceptualizations would not prove objectivity impossible any more than there being infinite possible classifications or descriptions. The objectivist can hold that the 'conceptualized perceptions' are various views of things, each view capable of being the common object of several different perceivers' attentions.

Perception and chaos

A third possible support for this selectivity of perception argument is suggested by Whorf when he talks of the 'kaleidoscopic flux,' and is also stated, not without ambiguity of intent, by Weber:

Life with its irrational reality and its store of possible meanings is inexhaustible. The *concrete* form in which value-relevance occurs remains perpetually in flux, ever subject to change in the dimly seen future of human culture. The light which emanates from those highest evaluative ideas always falls on an ever changing finite segment of the vast chaotic stream of events, which flows away through time.[17]

It is a well known popular thesis that nature is an unordered confusion out of which we 'carve' order for ourselves, and that this order carving is done at the level of perception. If, however, nature being in flux means that things change rapidly or that regularities are only approximate, then this is compatible with objectivity, since the extent to which and the time during which certain regularities do hold could, in principle, be objectively determined. But if nature being in flux means that there are *no* regularities, then the following situation seems to obtain: either that there are no regularities is to be taken to mean just that; or there is one subject matter exempt from this, namely the human acts of perceptual order creating.

Surely the perceptual relativist would not deny that at least people's acts of ordering are themselves ordered (if only qualifiedly and subject to change); since if there were no regularities in the order-creating process, it is hard to see how we could succeed in forging order out of the chaos we are supposed to confront. But can this much order be admitted? If human acts of ordering are not chaotic, why cannot other phenomena be likewise non-chaotic? Also it might be argued that, for social science at any rate, objective inquiry about what there is that is ordered would still be possible in the study of how people order the chaos confronting them.[18]

PERCEPTUAL INTERPRETATION

Arguments for perceptual relativism from the selectivity of perception are sometimes presented along with a not always distinguished and seldom worked out set of arguments having to do with interpretation. Polanyi in the passage above and Weber in some of his discussions talk of the interpretive nature of perception. Just what it is to say that perception is interpretive is not always clear, and arguments supporting this view which give it different senses can be divided into ones based on contradictory views: that there are sense data, and that there are not sense data.

Sense data

Supposing the first of these views, E.A. Burtt writes:

The fact is, we can mean by real objects only two things. They are either an entirely transcendent and unknowable x, about which nothing more can be said beyond the bare mention of them; or else they are constancies of relation between groups of sensed qualities. In the latter case they are objects of experience, and the space in which they exist is essentially identical with the space of perception. In common life we all assume this, and take for granted the general validity of judgments of location based on our own spatial perception.[19]

Burtt's view is, I think, that what we perceive are sensible qualities, appearances, or what are usually called sense data, and the passage here suggests two ways that the sense datum theory might give perceptual relativists a way of holding that perception is interpretive. One way is to take the position called representative realism and say that our perceiving just sense data requires us to infer the existence and qualities of ('transcendent')[20] objects from them. The other way is to embrace phenomenalism and argue that seeing 'objects' involves constructing them out of the sense data. Inferring and constructing could be said to be part of the perceptual process, thereby giving one sense to the perceptual relativist's claim.

One problem with appealing to the view of those sense datum theorists who advocate representative realism is that this view was put forth, by Russell for instance, to *preserve* objectivity, especially in science:

It is undeniable that our everyday interpretations of perceptive experiences, and even all our everyday words, embody theories. But it is not impossible to whittle away the element of interpretation, or to invent an artificial language involving a minimum of theory. By these methods we can approach asymptotically to the pure datum.[21]

Among the issues raised by this passage, one is especially noteworthy for present purposes. This is that in holding that there is interpretation involved somewhere in the perceptual process (where the limits of this process are loosely defined by both perceptual relativists and their opponents), Russell speaks of 'interpretations of perceptive experiences' rather than 'interpretive perceptions.' The force of the sense datum theory was to indicate a way that interpretations could be anchored in a non-interpretive base – something we 'know by acquaintance.'

Where then could the perceptual relativist find an element of perceptual interpretation in the sense datum view? Possibly in its claim that things and their qualities are inferred from sense data. Now one common criticism of sense datum theories is that in perceiving we do not infer from appearances that there are things and that they have certain qualities, at least not in the strict sense that we formulate to ourselves arguments with reports of our sense data as premises, and expressions about their causes as conclusions.[22]

A rejoinder to this is that the inferences may be considered as (usually) unconscious psychological processes. It could be held that our having perceptions causes us also to have certain beliefs about their causes, and that in retrospect and/or by some kind of 'reconstruction' we formulate arguments, the premises of which are reports of present or past sense data. Hence Russell talks of 'animal inferences' being habitual and unnoticed, and Moore of 'judgments of perception' in which we unconsciously frame beliefs about objects on the basis of sense data; and it does seem that even philosophers opposed to sense datum theories must agree that in this sense there can be 'inferences' of which we are not aware.[23] These inferences (conscious or not) are still, however, not interpretive perceptions but, if the representative realist's view is correct, perceptions and inferences. And the perceptions could still, at least in principle, serve as common observational bases after the interpretations have been stripped away.

The perceptual relativist might still argue that sense datum theories support his position (though not by giving him a suitable sense in which perceptions might be said to be interpretive), since consideration of the sense datum view brings to mind a much discussed philosophical puzzle. This is the long-standing problem of scepticism as regards agreement in perceptions. It is argued that some or all of our perceptions might be different (i.e., we have different sense data in the same circumstances – you see red, I see green), but it might be the case that they are so arranged that communication and cooperation would still be possible, so we could never find out whether we differed or not.

For present purposes I think that this problem can be avoided. In the first place, it would be difficult for the perceptual relativist to hold that this disparity could have any effect on scientific practice; since such an effect might offer scientists (or philosophers) a clue to the existence of this systematic disparity, and one of the suppositions of the problem (that there could be no way of detecting our perceptual differences in communication or practice) would not be fulfilled. In the second place, if we are to allow the possibility of there being undetectable but radical differences in perception to render some (at least perceptually based) beliefs unjustified, then it is hard to see how any such belief could be exempt, and this position would lead one toward thoroughgoing scepticism.

The doctrine of phenomenalism, that things and events are nothing but bundles of sense data and their relations, might be thought to offer another respect in which perception is interpretive. One could take the view of some phenomenalists that just what sense data are construed as constituting things and just what relations among sense data are selected as constituting events are determined by an often unconscious mental process of 'construction.' An appeal to phenomenalism, like an appeal to the argument about systematic perceptual disparity, confronts the problem of avoiding thoroughgoing scepticism. If pushed, the phenomenalist might have to deny that any beliefs are justified other than ones based on his own present perceptions, and this leads to solipsism, the view that only I (or my present perceptions) exist now, with its notoriously sceptical consequences.[24] But there is another difficulty.

Modern phenomenalists often advanced their view as a guarantee of scientific objectivity, precisely because they thought that scientific description and explanation (selective redescription in the phenomenalist view) could be firmly based in present (past, future, and possible) sense impressions. So if two persons unconsciously select the groupings of their perceptions differently, then, according to their theory, this would be a mere matter of convenience, and agreement on the most basic level – that concerning what present impressions there are – could always be reached in principle.

In *Sensationalism and Scientific Explanation* Peter Alexander criticizes phenomenalism for being out of accord with scientific explanation, arbitrary (since the success of predictions would be accidental), and excessively pragmatic (since distinctions like that between ourselves and the rest of the world would be matters of mere convenience).[25] And a standard criticism of phenomenalism is that it cannot explicate language referring to the conditions of perception requisite for making and testing predictions and sorting illusory from non-illusory perception, without regress.[26] Anti-objectivists might be tempted to argue that such criticisms show that the truth of phenomenalism would support anti-objectivism in the sciences despite the objectivist intentions of some of its adherents.

But this would seem to me to overlook the bases of the phenomenalist doctrine. The criticisms of phenomenalism mentioned urge either that the view is not in accord with our scientific and extra-scientific language or that it would make scientific explanation at least inordinately complex and perhaps impossible. The phenomenalist must meet these criticisms not just because he is a champion of objective science, but because to a great extent it is on the meanings of words in scientific and extra-scientific discourse and on considerations of economy in analyzing the structure of science that his position is based.[27] Hence the correctness of phenomenalism would tend to insure the adequacy of phenomenalism to account for scientific practice.

Seeing as

One interesting aspect of the arguments for perceptual relativism is that anti-objectivists have tried to defend it by appeal to the falsity of sense datum theories as well as to their truth. I believe this line of argument is what underlies Polanyi's explication of the interpretive element in perception. Citing Gestalt and transactional psychology, he claims that there is not only a selecting activity involved in perception, but also a 'shaping of percepts' according to our prior beliefs.[28]

Polanyi's reference to Gestalt psychology is representative of many perceptual relativist arguments. What is usually referred to by these appeals are the findings of Gestalt (and other) psychologists that there is a significant correlation between a person's beliefs and desires and the way he describes an ambiguous picture, or that there is a significant difference between the identifications of the same figure or object seen against different backgrounds. But, as noted above, such findings do not damage the objectivist's position, since he can admit such facts as that people are psychologically 'set' to notice certain things or interpret them in different ways.

However there is a philosophical point which these findings of Gestalt psychology can be taken to illustrate (even if some perceptual relativists try to rest too much on them). Two well known recent attacks on sense datum theories (both cited by perceptual relativists) are those of G.N.A. Vesey and Wittgenstein.[29] These attacks oppose to the knowledge-by-acquaintance doctrine of sense datum theorists the view that seeing is seeing as. As Vesey puts it:

'All seeing is seeing as.' In other words, if a person sees something at all it must look like something to him, even if it only looks like 'somebody doing something.' The less definite one's perception the less chance of its being non-veridical, but also the less chance of its being useful. Another way of expressing the point that all seeing is seeing as is to say that perceptions, like judgments, are either true or false. They are true when what the object looks like to somebody, that is, what on looking at it the person would take it to be if he had no reason to think otherwise, is what the object is; false otherwise.[30]

This view immediately generates another sense in which it might be said that perception is interpretive. It remains to be seen whether this would be a sense which would enable someone to defend perceptual relativism, if the view is correct.

It seems to me that the objectivist can accept the view expressed by Vesey. He can agree that two people A and B may be confronting the same object O, and that A sees it as an X and B as a Y. Since the objectivist can also hold that there is no reason in theory why A, for instance, could not also see O as a Y, or both 'interpret' O as a Z, and that there is no reason why, in the case where, because of a confirmed generalization or for logical reasons, both interpretations could not be correct, disputes about whether O has been correctly (or 'veridically') seen could not be settled by attaining closer perceptions of it, even if the number of such perceptions is indefinite. The objectivist's defence of his position here would be parallel to his defence of the compatibility of objectivity with an indefinite number of possible descriptions discussed above. He could point to his view's accord with the success of the experimental sciences and relative ease of human communication while challenging the perceptual relativist to avoid thoroughgoing scepticism.

An attempt to employ a bastard version of this theory is found in the late N.R. Hanson's application in his popular *Patterns of Discovery* of the view of Vesey and Wittgenstein to support his theory-ladenness argument. Since problems in his argument seem to me symptomatic of difficulties which face attempts to ground anti-objectivism in theories of perception generally, it will be instructive to examine Hanson's view. He says, in criticizing sense datum theorists:

To say that Tycho and Kepler, Simplicius and Galileo, Hooke and Newton ... all make the same observations but use them differently is too easy. It does not explain controversy in research science. Were there no sense in which they were different observations they could not be used differently.[31]

Again, discussing two disagreeing microbiologists looking in a micro-scope he holds:

Perhaps there is a sense in which two such observers do not see the same thing, do not begin from the same data, though their eyesight is normal and they are visually aware of the same object.[32]

And from considerations like these he concludes that 'there is a sense, then, in which seeing is a "theory-laden" undertaking. Observation of x is shaped by prior knowledge of x.'[33]

The cause of scientists' having different observations according to Hanson is that they have different interpretations of the subject matter observed, and seeing is interpretive: 'theories and interpretations are "there" in the seeing from the outset.' The main evidence that Hanson gives for this assertion is derived from reflection on such phenomena as ambiguous pictures, the 'spontaneous' ways that pictures of staircases 'go in reverse,' and some figures are seen now as representations of one thing, now of another, but not as both at once.[34]

But Hanson's general interpretation of perception is confused. He analyzes the concept of perceiving (he uses this term interchangeably with 'seeing') into 'visual awareness,' 'seeing as,' and 'seeing that.' Visual awareness is the awareness of what disagreeing perceivers do have in common. Thus Hanson maintains that when Tycho Brahe and Kepler looked at the sun, while one saw it as a globe circling the earth, the other as a globe around which the earth circles, 'something about their visual experiences at dawn is the same for both: a brilliant yellow-white disc ...' And, reproducing the well known ambiguous figure which can be seen as an old woman or as a young woman, he says that, even if we differ about what is represented, 'our sense-datum pictures must be the same ... the pictures we draw of what we see may turn out to be geometrically indistinguishable.'[35]

'Seeing as' and 'seeing that' are what 'bring' theories into our per-ceiving. A baby, in one of Hanson's favourite examples, could not see an object as an x-ray tube nor see that, were the object to be dropped, it would break. Of 'seeing that,' he says:

'Seeing that' threads knowledge into our seeing; it saves us from re-identifying everything that meets our eye ... The knowledge is there in the seeing and not an adjunct to it.[36]

So, because of their differing theories, 'Tycho and Simplicius see that the universe is geocentric; Kepler and Galileo see that it is heliocentric.'[37] (Of course if 'seeing that' is taken in the 'success sense' usually given it, then this passage must be understood to use 'see' in quotations, unless Hanson is here opting for thoroughgoing scepticism, contrary to his usual intent.)

To explain the mechanics of this 'threading' Hanson introduces the 'linguistic' dimension of knowing:

Our visual consciousness is dominated by pictures; scientific knowledge, however, is primarily linguistic. Seeing is ... an amalgam of the two – pictures and language. At the least, the concept of seeing embraces the concepts of visual sensation and of knowledge.[38]

Seeing, Hanson goes on to argue, is the bringing of linguistically contained knowledge to visual awareness to produce 'seeings that.'

What is supposed to make this whole view useful for supporting anti-objectivism is Hanson's treatment of visual awareness and its relation to 'seeing as' and 'seeing that.' But why, we might ask, cannot the visual awarenesses, which Hanson admits are the same for the two biologists, the baby and the scientist, and Tycho and Kepler, serve as a common perceptual meeting ground to aid in the settling of any disputes? Hanson's answer is that visual awareness alone, sense datum theorists (and his own occasional use of sense datum language) to the contrary, is not seeing at all unless it is conjoined with a linguistically conditioned 'seeing that.' Alone, visual awareness is undifferentiated, without any 'significance' or 'like the buzzing confusion of fainting.' The only ground for this view even hinted at by Hanson is in his analysis of the concept of 'seeing' which is supposed to reveal that while 'seeing that' is 'conceptual,' visual awareness is 'optical,' by which he seems to mean that visual awareness is merely physiological, having to do with retinal images and the like; while 'seeing is an experience ... a retinal reaction is only a physical state.'[39]

However part of the concept of 'seeing' is *not* that what Hanson calls 'visual awareness' is physiological, unlike what he calls 'seeing that.' Indeed many of Hanson's own descriptions of visual awareness include no specifically physiological language. Moreover, and this is the point of this discussion, a closer look at the examples Hanson gives of visual awareness shows that they too involve 'seeings as' and 'seeings that.' The two people who reproduce the ambiguous figure in drawings would both see their productions *as* drawings, not as, respectively, an actual young woman and an actual old woman. Both Tycho and Kepler, in their visual awarenesses of the sun on the horizon, would see it *as* three-dimensional, and they would see *that* they would fail to touch it should they reach out.

Hanson can derive anti-objectivist conclusions from his theory of perception because he analyzes perceiving in such a way that what he claims could only serve as common grounds of perceptual agreement between scientists (visual awareness) is not the kind of thing necessary to make agreement (or disagreement) in interpretations possible (for which 'seeing as' or 'seeing that' would be needed). To make a case for perceptual relativism, it has been necessary, so to speak, to 'mix up' different philosophical theories of perception. If, on the other hand, Hanson had remained true to his view that interpretations are 'there in the seeing from the outset,' and held that visual awarenesses are also 'seeings as,' the impediment to this possibility would have been removed.[40]

This does not mean that the possibility of perceptual agreement would be guaranteed or that perception would be infallible. It would not be infallible since, on the levels of visual awareness (however their boundaries are defined), the interpretive seeings might still be mistaken. It would not be guaranteed, because closer and closer inspection would also involve an element of interpretation, and there could be no guarantee of an ultimate court of appeal. But common perceptual ground is usually available, and to demand ultimate grounds while espousing a theory of perception such as the one under consideration is to take the first fatal step toward scepticism.

PERCEPTION AND THE WORLD

An especially interesting expression of the anti-objectivist view which turns to some theory of perception for support is one of Feyerabend's:

Nobody would dream of using the insight given by a new theory for the readjustment of some general beliefs only, leaving untouched the interpretation of the results of measurement. And nobody would dream of demanding that the meanings of observation statements as obtained with the help of measuring instruments remain invariant with respect to the change and progress of knowledge. Yet precisely this is done when the measuring instrument is a human being, and the indication is the behavior of this human being, or the sensations he has, at a particular time.[41]

I say that this defence of perceptual relativism is especially interesting, since there are some who espouse objectivism who also employ the heuristic device of comparing the human sensory apparatus to a measuring instrument,[42] and an examination of the appropriateness of this model will perhaps serve to summarize the objectivist position being urged here.

A moment's reflection shows why this comparison of the perceiving human with a scientific instrument is attractive to both the objectivist and the anti-objectivist. Anti-objectivists like it because instrument readings require interpretations by a scientist using a theory in order to be at all useful to him. The objectivist likes the comparison, since an instrument can, *prima facie*, aid one in discovering and recording actual properties of a subject matter, and one and the same instrument can record findings which can help to verify or falsify different theories.

We might crudely say that there are two connected machines, a sensing machine and an interpretation machine. In the anti-objectivist view the machines are so hooked up that the imputs of the sensing machine are crucially, if not wholly, dependent on the output of the interpreting machine. In the objectivist view the two machines are hooked up in such a way that either the inputs and outputs of the interpretation machine are dependent on the inputs of the sensing machine, or the two machines are so interlocked that there is, so to speak, mutual feedback between them, but the two together do in fact function in such a way as to yield (objectively) true information about the world. One might say that they function together to maintain equilibrium with their environment.

Adoption of one of these second, objectivist, models seems to me more probably justified. On the one hand, it allows for explanation of the relative success of the human sensing-interpreting apparatus in the (long-run and day-to-day) history of man's attempts to control his environment (and to communicate with others embarked on that attempt) – the fact of this success seems to me irrefutable on any basis short of thoroughgoing scepticism. And, on the other hand, arguments in favour of adopting the other model seem to me too weak to justify the startling claims that anyone accepting them would have to make.

Additionally anti-objectivists suppose that by showing that there is some element of selection or interpretation in perceptual experience or by showing that our perceptually gained beliefs are not objectively infallible, objectivism has been disproven. But the objectivist models *also* include interpreting machines (and selection, as has been noted, can easily be accommodated). And the objectivist need not maintain that the output of these machines is always reliable information, so long as in the long run the machines can adjust themselves to be generally reliable in reporting truths about the world.

CHAPTER FIVE

The social-scientific subject matter

Social theorists and philosophers of social science who are willing to admit the possibility of objectivity in the natural sciences sometimes withhold this possibility from the social sciences, appealing to the fact that humans are different from the objects of these other sciences. Now humans are indeed different from molecules or plants. That is to say, humans, considered as actors in social situations, have qualities not possessed by these kinds of objects and behave in ways that they do not. But neither of these characteristics alone makes anti-objectivism true of the social sciences, since such differences also exist among the objects of the non-social sciences. Molecules and plants also have very different qualities from one another and behave in very different ways. So the burden on the anti-objectivist is to show just what there is about human social agents that makes it impossible for us to describe or explain them objectively.

There are in fact several arguments. I think they can be divided into two general groups though they usually overlap in discussions by social theorists and philosophers of social science. One group focuses on the subject matter of the social sciences, the other on the fact that, in the case of the social sciences, both the subject of inquiry and the inquirers are the same kinds of things.

THE SUBJECT OF INQUIRY

Human uniqueness

A characteristic of humans sometimes mentioned in support of anti-objectivism is their uniqueness. Quentin Gibson notes that this sort of consideration cannot count against the possibility of objectivity; in order to know whether and how something is unique it is necessary to specify those respects which differentiate it from other things, and the anti-objectivist would surely not deny that the specification of at least these features could be objectively carried out.[1] The point can be developed by considering what it means to attribute uniqueness to something. Presumably it is to show dissimilarity from other things; but everything is similar to anything else in some respects and dissimilar in other respects, so the anti-objectivist using this argument would have to show just what kinds of dissimilarities make something unique and why it is that being unique in this way inhibits objectivity. Hence this argument from uniqueness is parasitic on other arguments which purport to show some special feature of the social-scientific subject matter.

A modified version of the uniqueness argument is that humans are different from all other subject matters in that anything less than a complete description fails to capture their true natures but that, because of the necessarily abstractive and selective characters of description (not to mention the practical problems involved in the endeavour), complete description is impossible; so what we have left are incomplete descriptions which falsify people's 'true' natures.[2] This way of construing the uniqueness argument does not take it very far. In some ways the argument resembles the infinity of selections argument examined in chapter 1 or the regress of possible descriptions argument examined in chapter 3. Even though a description of all of a person or group's characteristics is impossible, why cannot the descriptions which are made be objective, and why are fuller and fuller objective descriptions not possible? The anti-objectivist must show what there is about man's character that makes anything less than total description of him wholly inadequate, and this again would require some independent argument.

Human freedom

Some anti-objectivists appeal to the alleged freedom (in some anti-deterministic sense) of human agents.[3] This view has already been mentioned in chapter 1. It has to do not with the possibility of objectivity, but with the scope of social science. If some version of the anti-deterministic view were true, then at most only probabalistic laws would be possible in social science, and perhaps a strong enough version of indeterminism would necessitate that only description is possible. In either case the possibility of objectivity is not challenged, or at least not without adopting a certain doctrine about the 'meaningfulness' of human acts which will be examined below.

Human non-nature

There is a third argument in defence of anti-objectivism, perhaps a roundabout one, that should be mentioned. This is that the special nature of the social-scientific subject matter which makes objective study of it impossible is that it does not exist, and that hence *no* study of it is possible, and *a fortiori* no objective study. This, at least according to one of his critics, Peter Caws, is a central message of the structuralist Jacques Lacan when he says: 'There is no science of man, because the man of science does not exist, only its subject.'⁴ Caws interprets Lacan's view to mean that:

The subject is an activity, not a thing ... The idea that it had objective being and could be studied scientifically, according to Lacan, was a direct consequence of the success of science in throwing light on the rest of the world.⁵

This view is not altogether unique to structuralists. Jean-Paul Sartre is famous for denying that there is such a thing as human nature. Wilhelm Dilthey holds that individuals have 'meaning' (or their essential characters are created) in their relations to social-historical wholes, and, in language resembling that of modern structuralists, he further holds that individuals are points 'where systems intersect.' A view like this is also to be found in the writings of G.H. Mead, who sometimes speaks of social and natural 'processes' of which selves are just certain phases.⁶

A problem with theories like Lacan's, taken as defences of anti-objectivism, is seen if one attempts to understand their assertions that subjects do not exist. If 'subjects' means 'selves,' then in one way it is true that such arguments would deny the existence of selves as we usually think of them. But in another way the arguments do not deny the existence of selves; they just interpret them in certain ways – as purely receptive centres of consciousness, as the self-making agents described in Sartre's works, as points of intersection of systems, and as phases of processes. In any of these views objective study of selves would be possible (although for Lacan there might be a problem in explicating the mechanics of gaining this knowledge, but this is a special problem for structuralist methodology, not for objectivism).

Meaningful action

Max Weber made a basic distinction between 'meaningful action' and 'merely reactive behaviour,'⁷ thus carrying on a controversy in both philosophy and social theory, dating at least from the time of Kant, over the proper object of the human sciences. The debate has had the advantage of pressing social theorists rather deeply into methodological work and has contributed in recent years to a potentially fruitful interchange of ideas by social scientists and philosophers.

But it has also created the confusion mentioned in chapter 1, which only needs to be spelled out to be dissolved, but which continues to plague the objectivism–anti-objectivism controversy. This is that the two sides of the dispute often go by the names of 'subjectivism' and 'objectivism,' the former advocating that the proper study of social science is 'meaningful action,' the latter urging that external behaviour and/or the social-historical causes of both the behavioural and the mental are at least as important.[8] Because of the widespread nature of this confusion of 'subjectivism' with 'anti-objectivism'[9] it will be necessary to suggest some problems involved in the debate which might tempt one to see meaningfulness as that special quality of human activities which makes objective study of them impossible.

The nature of meaningful action (sometimes called 'action' as opposed to 'behaviour' or 'reaction') is not always clearly spelled out by its advocates or opponents. Ludwig von Mises defines it:

Human action is purposeful behavior. Or we may say: action is will put into operation and transformed into agency, is aiming at ends and goals, is the ego's meaningful response to stimuli and to the conditions of its environment, is a person's conscious adjustment to the state of the universe that determines his life.[10]

Here von Mises combines several senses of 'meaningful action,' but since slightly different problems are involved when different groups of senses are considered, it will be helpful to sort them out.

1 Human action (and possibly some animal behaviour, though action theorists are in disagreement on this point) is said by some, like F.A. Hayek, Alfred Schutz, and Florian Znaniecki,[11] to be interpretive activity. As MacIver puts it: 'The social phenomenon ... is always a mental response to a complex situation selectively conceived.'[12] What is being urged is that humans act on their interpretations of external stimuli, and explanations of action must take into account this interpretation (sometimes called the 'humanistic coefficient').

2 Talcott Parsons includes as part of the meaning of 'act' that it must be purposive: 'For purposes of definition the act must have an "end," a future state of affairs toward which the process of action is oriented.'[13] This view is also held by von Mises who, like Weber, ties the purposiveness of action to the concept of a rational action,' or one in which an agent adjusts his activity to attaining certain goals.[14]

3 Closely related to the purposiveness interpretation is the Weberian view discussed in chapter 1 that 'evaluation' is what sets human activity apart. Humans alone act in accord with values.

4 Also related to 2 is the view that human action is irreducibly 'inten-

tional,' a view advanced among others by G.E.M. Anscombe, A.I. Melden, and Stuart Hampshire.[15]

5 Peter Winch has argued in his book *The Idea of a Social Science* that humans cannot be understood as behaving in response to causes, but must be seen as acting in accord with conventions or rules.[16] This view is also espoused by R.S. Peters: 'The job of anthropologists and sociologists, to a large extent, is to exhibit the structure of goals and conventions in unfamiliar societies.'[17]

6 Another interpretation of meaningful action is that humans act in accord with reasons, where reasons are construed not as causes but as one's purposes and the plans of action he follows in pursuing them. This view is usually put forth by philosophers of history such as R.G. Collingwood and William Dray, but is also employed by some philosophers of social science.[18]

The concept of meaningful action, in one or more of its interpretations, is linked with other views of the special nature of the social-scientific subject matter. For instance, Parsons, Winch, Collingwood, and Hampshire link this view with indeterminism, arguing that purposive, rule-governed, or reason-guided actions must in some indeterministic sense be 'free' actions. There is a certain coherence among the various interpretations of what meaningful acts are, but three separate problems are raised by focusing on different ones.

Interpretive action and behaviourism Meaningful action considered as interpretive involves mental events which are not externally observable. Hence it is not surprising that advocates of the view that such action is the proper object of social-scientific inquiry should oppose behaviourism. Stephen Strasser's main targets for attack are Tolman and Skinner, and Alfred Schutz maintains that all 'naturalistic' approaches in social science, being concerned just with 'overt behavior,' have their 'logical conclusion' in psychological behaviourism.[19]

In a passage typical of subjectivist attacks on psychological behaviourism MacIver writes:

The forces which combine to produce a physical phenomenon are unified outside our recognition of them. The unity is objective, and the relations of the determinants are, therefore, amenable to objective methods of investigation ...The forces which combine to produce a social phenomenon are to begin with of a totally different order, since they are all construed as aspects of experience, and they are unified, in producing the phenomenon, only within and through the mentality which experiences them. The unity is subjective, and the relative impacts of the determinants ... are made no longer on one another as in the physical process but on the active mentality ... If we realize this truth we see how vain, in fact how ludicrous is the project of a behavioristic sociology. Incompetent to deal with the subjectivity of experience the behaviorists would discard it altogether.[20]

This passage is typical in that it suggests as exhaustive alternatives on the one hand a subjectivist approach which sees the mental unification of experience, not accessible to the methods of observation of the physical sciences, as the proper object of inquiry, and on the other hand a behaviourism which banishes all reference to anything that cannot be directly observed and measured. There are several problems with such a view. The major one is that not all anti-subjectivists are or need be behaviourists. Theorists otherwise as different as Freudians and speculative physiological psychologists in the materialist tradition reject the subjectivist focus on the 'meaningful,' but equally reject the anti-theoretical inductivist temper and deliberately piecemeal approach of most behaviourists. But in addition it is not obvious that actual behaviourism cannot account for the realm of interpretive action, or at least subjectivist arguments to this effect are typically inconclusive.

Behaviourism can be taken as advocating a strong or a weak thesis. As a strong thesis behaviourism does indeed prescribe that only references to overt, and perhaps also even non-verbal, responses are to be admitted in scientific explanations of human behaviour. As a weaker thesis it holds that, while reference to intervening, mental variables may be admitted in explanation, mental event or state terms must be linked with behaviour at least at some points by means of operational definitions or, even less strictly, by employing bridge laws connecting mental and non-mental occurrences.[21]

Another criticism of subjectivist attacks on behaviourism is that they take only its strong version (sometimes called 'radical behaviourism') to task, ignoring the more moderate version (and the one more in vogue today) which need not deny the existence of the mental states and events involved in the kinds of explanations prescribed by subjectivists. And a third problem is the almost cavalier dismissal of behaviourism even in its strong sense. A radical behavourist need not deny that human activity involves interpretation as long as he can also hold that it is at least possible in principle to break the concept of 'interpretation' down entirely into concepts (like 'belief' and 'desire') which he thinks can in turn be operationally defined.[22]

Yet another problem with anti-objectivist arguments which appeal to anti-behaviourism (related to the first problem) is that they tend to assume the excessively tight requirements placed on verifications by the very forms of behaviourism they attack. For instance, Hayek states:

We know ... that in his conscious decisions man classifies external stimuli in a way which we know solely from our own subjective experience of this kind of classification. We take it for granted that other men treat various things as alike or unlike just as we do, although no objective test, no knowledge of the relations of these things to other parts of the external world justifies this.

But in the very next sentence Hayek suggests a way in which we *can* gain objective beliefs about these things:

Our procedure is based on the experience that other people as a rule (though not always – e.g., not if they are color-blind or mad) classify their sense impressions as we do.[23]

Hayek's use of classification as his example of interpretive activity is a bit loaded, since he also holds the view examined already that systems of classification, being arbitrary, are non-objective, But his comment suggests one way that objective belief about mental events is possible; namely, by inferences employing analogical reasoning based on experience.

Why does Hayek want to disallow that such analogical reasoning could be objective? Madmen and colour-blind people are excluded presumably on objectively ascertainable grounds. In the one case we know for physiological and psychological reasons that the experiences of a colour-blind person will differ from ours in some respects. In the other case we have observed behaviour so grossly incompatible with our own, in similar circumstances, that we may infer that the processes of interpretation by such people are very probably different. The fact that this knowledge is inferential and only probable could be seen as a hindrance to objectivity only by someone who demanded the certainty of all social-scientific conclusions. The point here is that, whether one abandons or modifies strong behaviourism, he can hold that these acts of interpretation are accessible to objective study, even though they are not accessible to direct observation (unless, of course, we are to count knowledge of our own acts of interpretation as knowledge by observation) and even though inferences about them are not certain. In demanding certainty the advocates of this sort of argument demand too much.

Another example of this excessive demand is seen in MacIver's comment about measurement. It is true that precise measurement of the complex mental acts of interpretation which the subjectivists have in mind is probably not possible now or in the foreseeable future. But in the first place, measurability is not a requirement of objectivity for any science (although it is, no doubt, desirable). And in the second place, it is not true that all mental phenomena are in principle incapable of measurement. Work in the techniques of constructing questionnaires and opinion polls and in analyzing their results has surely made some inroads into the measurement of attitudes, and work like that of Lazarsfeld in the mathematical expression of underlying attitudes and beliefs surely cannot be altogether discounted.[24] It has even been argued that recent advances in experimental and measurement techniques of both subjectivist and non-subjectivist theorists have all but dissolved the general dispute between them regarding the proper tasks of social inquiry.[25]

Purposes and values Meaningful acts considered as intentional, evaluative, or purposive might be thought to pose a special problem for the objectivist. Such acts are subject to various mutually exclusive descriptions (for an external observer at any rate), and it is sometimes argued that there is no way of determining just which description is correct. Much of this dispute revolves around debates in philosophical psychology over the nature of practical reasoning, the logic of act description and explanation, the status of intentions, and so on. But in relation to the objectivism–anti-objectivism controversy I do not think there is a serious difficulty.

The problem about descriptions is generated in two ways.[26] One is that, since not all acts intentionally carried out (or directed at achieving some purpose) succeed, and since one's verbal reports of his own intentions are untrustworthy, giving a correct description of an act is problematic, and some participants in this dispute hold that there is no way of singling out one act description as the correct one. The second way the problem is generated is by considerations like those of Eric D'Arcy that one and the same act may be subject to many different descriptions depending on the interests of the describer. Both these problems seem to me to reduce to other problems. The first is clearly a species of the problem about verification just discussed. What makes it plausible is the supposition that knowledge of others' intentions, purposes, etc., must be direct and certain.

The second problem reduces, on the one hand, to the problems, discussed in chapters 3 and 4, of the possibly indefinite number of descriptions of or perspectives on a thing. There it was argued that the mere possibility of such multiple description or perception does not militate against objectivity. On the other hand, insofar as this possibility is grounded in the nature of intentional action – that is, insofar as a person can truly be said to be doing more than one thing (e.g., one may intentionally do x in order to get Y) – this is not a difficulty for the objectivist, but for philosophers facing other problems, e.g., of legal philosophy. Indeed it arises because the various, non-mutually exclusive descriptions can be known to be (objectively) true.

A similar point can be made about rule-following explanations. The concept of a rule is far from unambiguous as it is used by social theorists and philosophers of social science.[27] Insofar as a problem for objectivism is involved, it would presumably be, again, that it is impossible to determine with certainty what conventions or rules someone was following (since a rule can always be violated, and awareness of rules is subjective).

Reasons and explanation Another philosophical problem comes to mind in the case of meaningful actions interpreted as purposive or reason-guided as opposed to caused, in that many philosophers have urged that explanations in terms of purposes and by reference to reasons differ essentially from other explanations. Hence Charles Taylor argues that explanations in terms of purposes are irreducibly teleological, and social philosophers like Richard Taylor, Peters, Melden, and Winch and philosophers of history like Dray offer various arguments that explanation in terms of reasons (Melden uses 'motives') is of a different kind from explanations in terms of causes or from those employing 'covering laws' of any kind.[28] Dray's view of such explanation, often now called 'rational explanation,' is representative:

The goal of such explanation is to show that what was done was the thing to have done for the reasons given, rather than merely the thing that is done such occasions, perhaps in accordance with certain laws (loose or otherwise).[29]

Now much debate surrounds the views of Charles Taylor, Dray, and the others. Taylor's view is challenged both on the grounds that teleological explanation is not especially suited to explanation in the social sciences and also on the grounds that all teleological explanation is reducible in principle to mechanical explanation.[30] Rational explanation is likewise surrounded by debate. Philosophers have argued that reasons *can* be causes, and practically every philosopher who has written on the topic takes up the debate between Dray and Hempel on the question of whether rational explanation can be construed as a special case of 'covering-law' explanation.[31]

These debates, however, relate, not to the possibility of the objectivity of social-scientific conclusions, but to the structure of explanations which are supposed to yield those conclusions. The point is obscured because advocates of meaningful-action explanation in the senses discussed are loathe to employ terms like 'objective' because of the confusion in the literature between 'objective' and 'object' as in 'physical object.' Also objectivist opponents of this view sometimes maintain that the reason they defend the methods of natural science as appropriate to the social ones is because they believe that only in that way can objective conclusions be reached. But this is predicated on the correctness of their view of social-scientific (and historical) explanation. Were the teleological and rationalizing views of explanation correct, then surely it would be open to their adherents to hold that the conclusions reached by them were objective.

Indeed, aside from his reservations about the effect of values in specifically historical explanation, Dray seems to endorse the objectivist view regarding the amassing of evidence.[32] I see no reason why it could not be determined objectively whether a certain person acts out of a certain reason and whether (and in what way) a person's acts tend to realize a certain purpose.[33] The point is a general one for these arguments from meaningful action. Unless arguments independent of them are employed, then what intentions, purposes, and valued goals people have, how they interpret the world, what rules or conventions they follow, and what reasons they act in accord with are all of them determinable (with more or less probability) objectively.

THE INQUIRER AND HIS SUBJECT

Many social theorists make much of the fact that in the social sciences the scientist and his subject-matter, the student and the studied, are the same kinds of things; both are social, human beings. Of course other sciences share this characteristic to some extent. Biologists, for instance, are themselves living organisms.[34] But it might be said that in the social sciences the inquirer shares more qualities with the subject of his inquiry than in other sciences. This fact creates special problems for the social scientist in neutralizing the effects of bias and in making up for the limitations on experimentation dictated by moral considerations. It also creates the interactions between social-scientific work and other social activities which have provided interesting subject matter for the historian and the student of social dynamics.

The question pertinent to the present discussion is why this characteristic of the social sciences should be thought to support anti-objectivism. I find several groups of answers to this question. Some arguments focus on the fact that social scientists have values, thus resting the case on the arguments from values examined in chapter 1. The remaining ones include what might be called the arguments from participant observation, the self-fulfilling (or self-defeating) prediction arguments, arguments for the limitations of *Verstehen*, and some modifications of historicism.

Participant observation

The first of these arguments has to do with the interaction of the social scientist and his subject matter made possible by their both being humans. The argument can take two forms (though only one of them is prominent in contemporary discussions). John Madge summarizes one:

Today the widespread use of active interventionist techniques demands very carefully consideration of the effect of interaction between observer and observed. Any participation of the observer in social processes must lead to some modification of these processes; if it is agreed, as has been suggested, that the observer must participate in order to achieve insight, then the observed situation is bound to differ from the unobserved situation.[35]

The interaction can, as theorists in the Freudian tradition have noted, also have effects which work the other way. The observer might become so immersed in the social life of his subjects that *he* is unduly influenced by their beliefs about themselves and about him.

On the face of it these arguments might indeed be thought to support anti-objectivism. If the social scientist's very presence as an observer changes the situation observed, then anti-objectivism as defined in this work might seem to follow directly. As Madge puts it 'the fact of observation itself modifies the situation being observed.' And if a social scientist were to become so immersed in his subject matter that he took over his subject's beliefs, then objectivism would seem to be possible only if the subjects studied happened to hold objectively true beliefs about themselves (and what guarantee could there be of this, short, perhaps, of an argument that people are and are only what they believe themselves to be?).[36]

On examination, however, the first version ends up being not incompatible with objectivism. It is not that the thoughts and experiences of the social scientist are somehow formed or determined in the machinery of his explanation in such a way that two scientists with different theories, languages, and so on, could never come to agreement. It is that the subject matter he addresses is always influenced by his physical presence. It is for this reason that Nagel and others see no difference in principle between this kind of interaction and the interaction of the subject matters of other sciences with the instruments used to measure them.[37] It might be urged that different social scientists differently affect the same situations, but, even if there were a significant difference, this itself could be objectively determined and allowed for. Different scientists could compare their (objective) findings in such situations.

Even if participant observation were the only means of gaining social-scientific data, objectivism would still be possible (though if this were the only method, it would limit the scope of objective social-scientific conclusions, since allowing for the presence of the observing scientist would require theoretical work drawing on more sources and with independent validation). However it is often noted that there are other ways of gaining data in the social sciences. Participant observation can be supplemented with statistical comparisons and the results of unobserved observation. In fact some social scientists hold that participant observation should be subordinate to these other methods, entering into research, if at all, as a heuristic device for suggesting problems and hypotheses.[38] Moreover not a little work has been done by social scientists in finding techniques for either minimizing the effects of an observer's presence (like prolonged observation and special training in interviewing techniques) or allowing for them (e.g., by finding ways to determine the attitudes of the subject being interviewed toward the interviewer).[39]

An argument for anti-objectivism based on the fact of interaction where the effects of interaction run the other way, from subject to scientist, faces different but no less serious problems. In the first place it supposes a dubious view of role adoption – that while adopting the role of a participant in some activity we cannot also maintain traits associated with other roles, like those of a scientist.[40] Additionally it is hard to see just what the basis of such a view could be. If it were based on empirical investigation, the view is in danger of being self-defeating (if the investigation involved interviews) or of admitting that there are more ways than one of gaining reliable social-scientific conclusions (if the investigation did not involve interviews).

Self-fulfilling predictions

Another kind of argument appeals to the well known examples of self-fulfilling and suicidal predictions. R.K. Merton notes that 'prophecies,' though baseless, may become true just by being made (announcing that a bank, though financially sound, is about to be overdrawn may cause a run in which this actually occurs). He sees it as a 'paradox' that a prediction

... if it is made public ... becomes seemingly invalidated, and if it is not made public, it is generally regarded not as a prediction but as a postdiction. It is considered knowledge after the fact.[41]

And many theorists (posssibly including Merton, though in the example of the bank he is more interested in the way prejudices are reinforced) have seen here a threat to objectivity.

Now the view that this state of affairs is unique to the social sciences has been debated, as has the view that predictions are therefore invalidated in social science. Adolf Grünbaum advances a standard objectivist position regarding the latter view in arguing that social predictions 'are predicated on the prior fulfilment of certain initial conditions which include the presence in the society of men who are dissatisfied' and would, therefore, act on certain social-scientific views if they became known to them.[42] Even aside from Grünbaum's point, this argument does not support anti-objectivism, but instead requires objectivity. The reason that a social scientist worrying about the possibilities raised by Merton might feel qualms about making a certain prediction public is that he can predict that the making public of the prediction is likely to have certain effects (a prediction, it should be noted, which could only itself be construed in turn as self-fulfilling or suicidal under the most unlikely circumstances, e.g., that the members of the scientist's society had overwhelming desires to satisfy or to thwart his predictions). Similarly the fact that even groundless prophecies of bank runs, for example, can cause bank runs is itself known (non-groundlessly) by economists and bankers.

The limitations of Verstehen

A third group of arguments for anti-objectivism hinging on the fact that both the social scientist and his subject matter are humans might be called the 'limitations of *Verstehen*' argument. Hayek writes:

The sole difference between mind and physical objects ... which entitles us to speak of mind at all, is precisely that wherever we speak of mind we interpret what we observe in terms of categories which we know only because they are the categories in which our own mind operates.[43]

This is coupled with the view that the proper subject matter of social science is what Hayek calls 'mind' ('meaningful action' in one interpretation) and the view that we come to an understanding of social phenomena only by means of comparing others' experiences with our own (at the least) and imaginatively experiencing them ourselves (at the most). Reflections such as Hayek's generate some arguments which claim to show at least severe limitations on what can be objectively known.

A usual argument regarding understanding of this kind, called *Verstehen* by Weberians,[44] is that, if a social scientist has not had certain kinds of experiences, then he cannot hope to understand the actions of those who have. But another way that objectivity might be inhibited if *Verstehen* was the only means of gaining social-scientific knowledge is that the social scientist might illegitimately interpret some subject's experiences according to 'categories' familiar to him but foreign to his subjects. Indeed if this was the *only* social-scientific method, it would be quite difficult to avoid this.

It is noteworthy that these arguments suppose both that meaningful action is the proper subject matter of social science and that *Verstehen* is the only means of coming to any conclusions about that subject matter. It should also be noted that treatments of the concept of *Verstehen* are far from clear. It is not clear whether '*Verstehen*' is supposed to refer to a heuristic device for suggesting hypotheses, as many critics of approaches based on it hold, or whether it is itself supposed to be a kind of special understanding similar to what Collingwood calls 're-enactment,' or whether it is a means of validation – or else some combination of these.[45] However most of these problems have to do with the explanatory force, if any, of *Verstehen,* and we are here interested in the possibility of objectivity in making social-scientific descriptions and conclusions. In any case, the limitation of *Verstehen* argument must be met, regardless of the exact nature of the concept.

The projection of meaning One argument that *Verstehen* inhibits objectivity is found, in seed, in the writings of Schutz. He argues both that *Verstehen* is essential to social-scientific thought in order to identify people's meaningful acts, and that social scientists as well as their subjects think in terms of 'common-sense' constructs which are formed 'relatively to their biographical situations.'[46] An extension of this is that in understanding (constructing) the meaningful action of someone with a very different kind of biography from us, we may impose our way of acting meaningfully on him, and there may be no way of discovering whether this has been done. Schutz himself recognizes this sort of problem and tries to solve it by advocating that *Verstehen* be supplemented by another Weberian device, ideal type analysis, or the construction of models of meaningful action with 'typical' motives, goals, etc.[47] This does not solve the problem, of course, since an anti-objectivist can claim that one's system of 'constructs' would also determine what he considers typical.

A version of this problem is also noted by Ernest Gellner in connection with the disputes among anthropologists over how to interpret charitably the actions and assertions of members of primitive societies.[48] The problem might be put this way; in trying to establish the beliefs of peoples on little evidence, anthropologists employ a principle of assuming their subjects to be sane (in the absence of evidence to the contrary). However if the standards of sanity differed for the scientists from different cultures, then two anthropologists might be equally justified in interpreting the same actions in different ways on the same evidence.

Both these versions of this problem depend upon the impossibility of the social scientist's having *objective* principles for determining modes of typical action or sanity. That is, the assumption behind this version of the limitations of *Verstehen* argument is that the reason social scientists are in danger of reading their own interpretations, standards of conduct, and so on, into the actions of others is that these very interpretations and standards determine their way of thinking about their subject matter, and there is no way of objectively evaluating the interpretations and standards. But then independent defence of this view is needed, and it would, I believe, lead someone advocating it to one of the more general anti-objectivist arguments discussed in the previous chapters.

Perhaps an example of this can be seen in an argument sometimes advanced by students of symbolic interactionism and, to the extent that this theory has a philosophical analogue in phenomenology,[49] also by phenomenologists. According to the symbolic interactionist,[50] things are experienced (in everyday life and in scientific inquiry) in accord with plans of action bound up with the use of certain symbols ('symbolic representations of possibilities'). For instance, a piece of chalk as a possible writing implement and as a possible missile would be seen differently. But then, it might be argued, the social scientist could not avoid constructing the systems of symbolic representation of possible subjects of his social-scientific inquiries in accord with his own system, any more than he could avoid this regarding any other object of his attention. Hence, two social scientists with different systems of representation could never come to objective agreement.

This argument faces several problems. One is that it is in danger of being self-defeating, since symbolic interactionists, like Herbert Blumer, claim that their basic tenets are empirically verified, and phenomenologists (at least those who follow the mainstream of Husserl's thought) claim not only that the basic views of phenomenology are objectively true, but that it is only by following the methods of phenomenology that (objective) bases for philosophical and scientific inquiry can be secured.[51]

In addition to this difficulty, symbolic interactionism, if it were the best social-scientific approach, would guarantee at least the possibility of overcoming such an impediment to objective agreement. According to this theory it is a necessary condition of one's having plans of action and systems of symbolic representation that he be able to adopt the roles (including the systems of representation) of others.[52] So there would be nothing in principle to prevent scientists from coming to agreement by adopting various roles, including one another's and the roles of their subjects of inquiry. Strengthening this argument would, then, require turning to the general anti-objectivist arguments discussed in earlier chapters (perhaps those for perceptual relativism).

Reliving The more common limitation of *Verstehen* argument is that we cannot identify or in some sense understand another's meaningful actions by reliving, empathizing with, or imaginatively reproducing his experiences if we ourselves have not had similar experiences. So while (objectively) justified beliefs might be possible about those who have faced problems similar to ones we have faced and gone about solving them in similar ways, there is no possibility of gaining any knowledge about others, except by the 'external' behaviouristic means (which on this view would be inadequate to the study of meaningful action). In one respect this argument is not so much directed against objectivism as it is designed to narrow the scope of social-scientific inquiry. But it should still be examined, partly because it would so drastically narrow the scope of inquiry, and partly because objectivity regarding any description and explanation employing this method alone would be hard to ascertain, because of the difficulty of setting criteria for legitimate *Verstehen*.

Advocates of *Verstehen* are not always clear about just what it is that we must relive in order to recognize and/or explain the meaningful actions of others. It is suggested by some theorists, like Hayek and Znaniecki (though neither is consistent) that the social scientist must actually have just the same sorts of thoughts and desires as his subject, much as Collingwood held that this was necessary for the historian.[53] In an extreme version of this view a sociologist who did not suffer from racial hatred, or at least who could not imagine himself into the frame of mind of the bigot, could not truly understand the latter's actions.

A slightly different view of what it is that must be shared by the social scientist and his subject is held by Winch. He thinks that it is necessary for the social scientist to have participated in the same kind of rule-governed activity as his subject. For Winch meaningful behaviour, as opposed to reactive behaviour, is characterized by acting in accord with rules, and different sorts of rules are appropriate to different sorts of activities, e.g., to the activities of religious worship or artistic creation. Winch's argument relevant to the present discussion is that someone unacquainted with these rules at first hand could not hope to come to an understanding of the activities governed by them. And it is in the light of his theory about rules that he interprets 'such common-sense considerations' as that

... a historian or sociologist of religion must himself have some religious feeling if he is to make sense of the religious movement he is studying and understand the considerations which govern the lives of its participants. A historian of art must have some aesthetic sense if he is to understand the problems confronting the artists of his period; and without this he will have left out of his account precisely what would have made it a history of *art*, as opposed to a rather puzzling external account of certain motions which certain people have been perceived to go through.[54]

A third view of what it is that we must identify with is suggested by Weber:

In the same way [that we understand what someone is doing when he carries out a train of formal reasoning] we also understand what a person is doing when he tries to achieve certain ends by choosing appropriate means on the basis of the facts of the situation as experience has accustomed us to interpret them.

Such an interpretation of this type of rationally purposeful action possesses, for the understanding of the choice of means, the highest degree of verifiable certainty.[55]

Weber here sets up a kind of scale of *Verstehen* graduated according to the specificity of what is shared by social scientist and subject. This suggests that at the lowest end of this scale (perhaps Weber's 'purely intellectual understanding') the social scientist need only have experienced rational, purposive activity of some sort or another, not have pursued the very same ends and entertained the same means as the subjects of his study.

On the first of these views of what is understood the *Verstehen* position is sometimes attacked for committing what Rudner and others call the 'reproductive fallacy'; that is, it confuses describing or explaining some experience with having the experience:

... this error rests on a confusion between a description and what is described. Albert Einstein once remarked, it is not the function of science 'to *give* the taste of the soup.' To be a description of the taste of soup is clearly not to *be* the taste of soup.[56]

This criticism seems to me to point in the right direction. But possibly a *Verstehen* advocate would not be very distressed by it, since he holds not that reliving is describing, but that it is a necessary condition for describing. Only after having empathetically understood some act is one provided with the correct categories for describing and explaining it.

Gibson suggests one way that the objectivist criticism can be strengthened. He criticizes advocates of the 'imaginative identification' view for being unclear on whether they maintain that we gain understanding by imagining how *we* would feel in the circumstances confronting a subject of inquiry or by imaginatively reproducing in ourselves feelings very similar to those the subject himself has had, given *his* personality.[57] If advocates of *Verstehen* mean the former, then the problem of the limitations of *Verstehen* is not whether the social scientist can have his subject's actual thoughts, but whether he has been in or can imaginatively place himself in the same circumstances as his subjects of inquiry.

It is on this interpretation that *Verstehen* is seen by Gibson and others as a heuristic device for suggesting what might have motivated someone in a certain circumstance, by using the assumption that his reactions are similar to the social scientist's. This assumption may turn out to be false (it might be found that in circumstances similar to ones the social scientist has been in, the subject regularly acts differently). So hypotheses based on the assumption may fail, and this failure might be said to be due to the fact that the social scientist's ways of reacting to things is different from his subject-matter's. But this would not mean that the social scientist could not understand the subject's actions. It would only mean that he would have to try out other hypotheses as to the subject's probable reactions to such situations.

If *Verstehen* advocates hold the second view suggested by Gibson, that the social scientist must be able to reproduce the sorts of feelings, etc., the *subject* would have, then Gibson notes that independent evidence would be required for determining what sort of person the subject is. On this second interpretation the indispensable need for *Verstehen* is eliminated, since the independent means required to identify the sorts of feelings, etc., which that kind of subject has in principle, replaces *Verstehen* in the social scientist's inquiries. What might remain is the need for having thoughts, etc., similar to the subject in order to sympathize with him (perhaps to check a tendency toward bias).

This counter-argument is designed to show that *Verstehen*, interpreted in the narrow sense under discussion, is by itself inadequate to the task of gaining social-scientific knowledge. And it seems to me that the argument might go some way toward alerting advocates of *Verstehen* to the danger of overenthusiasm about the method they espouse. But to an anti-objectivist – one primarily concerned to disprove the possibility of (objective) social-scientific knowledge – the argument might be taken to show just how limited *Verstehen* is. And if he also held that the only possible means for gaining social-scientific knowledge is *Verstehen*, then he might welcome Gibson's argument as support for his anti-objectivist conclusion.

But now it would be incumbent on the anti-objectivist to support the view that *Verstehen*, as in this interpretation, *is* absolutely requisite for identification or understanding in the social sciences. He would have to give reasons for believing the proposition (a counter-factual one for him) that, were social-scientific knowledge possible, it would require the social scientist's having had (or being able somehow to induce in himself) the same sorts of beliefs and desires as those of the subjects he wants to understand. I do not see how this position could be defended.

It seems in the first place at best a questionable and at worst simply an arbitrary thesis that only if a social scientist has had certain thoughts and feelings can he either recognize the external manifestations of such thoughts and feelings (presumably what is meant by saying that *Verstehen* is requisite for identification or description) or explain a subject's behaviour by reference to his mental history (the elements of which the social scientist must presumably also have shared). It is doubtful that anybody has exactly the same sorts of desires and beliefs as someone else in the way claimed to be requisite for these tasks, if for no other reason than that overt actions are seldom correlated with single desires, but with whole packages of desires, thoughts, etc. So to hold strictly to the thesis under question, it would be necessary to maintain that the social scientist would need to have not only the same sorts of feelings and beliefs, but the same packages of them – and perhaps acquired in the same order and with the same intensity.

Indeed it is hard to see where a limit could be drawn to rule out the need for the social scientist to have had the very same mental history as his subjects. Clearly such a requirement is too strict. We can empathize with people whose mental lives have not been altogether parallel to ours, and, whatever the relation of empathy to *Verstehen,* surely our ability to gain the former is at least correlated with our ability to gain the latter.

In the light of this *prima facie* evidence against a view based on this strict *Verstehen* requirement, the anti-objectivist might try to loosen the restrictions. But in addition to facing the problem of finding criteria for placing limits on the degree of similarity requisite for *Verstehen,* such loosening would seem to move his position toward one of the less narrow interpretations of the *Verstehen* doctrine discussed below. The anti-objectivist might alternatively argue that it is part of the meaning of 'social-scientific understanding' (or 'description') that it involves *Verstehen* in the strict and narrow sense, that a social scientist who cannot at least imaginatively reconstruct the mental history of his subject has not really understood (or recognized) the subject's actions.

This, in fact, is the sort of argument with which philosophers of history in the Collingwood tradition marshall support for Collingwood's claim about the special place of 'reliving' in historical explanation.[58] This seems to me at least a debatable thesis about explanation in the work of historians. But it would certainly be a weak argument as applied to disciplines like sociology and economics which are unquestionably part of the social sciences (unlike history, according to Collingwoodians). Because comparatively little actual social-scientific description and explanation proceed as *Verstehen* advocates say it should, such a defence would rest on stipulative definitions of phrases like 'social-scientific understanding.' And adopting these definitions would itself require justification.

Winch's argument about rules may involve similar problems, but additional considerations are in order. Winch has two grounds for saying that a social scientist must have participated in the same kinds of rule-governed activities as those he studies. One, taken over with some modification from Michael Oakeshott, is that no purposive action takes place in a social vacuum, and we must know the social circumstances in order to understand acts of people in them:

> ... both the ends sought and the means employed in human life, so far from generating forms of social activity, depend for their very being on those forms. A religious mystic, for instance, who says that his aim is union with God, can be understood only by someone who is acquainted with the religious tradition in the context of which this end is sought ... [59]

On one interpretation this can be admitted without also admitting Winch's argument that we have to have experienced the religious tradition in the sense of having been religious. Being 'acquainted with' in this passage might simply mean 'having studied,' and few social scientists would deny that one cannot properly understand a person's activity without studying his social environment.

The second ground for Winch's argument is that acting in a social context is following conventional rules of behaviour, as opposed to habitually responding to social stimuli. Then, citing Wittgenstein, Winch argues that we can only know these rules if we can ourselves follow them, and this requires actually participating in the activities which are guided by them.[60] It seems to me, however, that it is possible to know that a person is following a certain kind of rule without knowing the exact rule. To take the example which Winch borrows from Wittgenstein, without knowing which rule a person is following it is possible to know that he is uttering names of numbers according to *some* complicated rule of arithmetic progression, and thereby to understand, for instance, why he hesitated at first but responded quite rapidly later. And it also seems that somebody can learn (though perhaps with greater effort) the conventional rules of some social procedure without participating in them by observing regularities and asking people what they would do in certain circumstances.

Winch's implied rejoinder to both objections can be seen in his example of prayer:

> ... what the sociologist is studying, as well as his study of it, is a human activity and is therefore carried on according to rules. And it is these rules, rather than those which govern the sociologist's investigation, which specify what is to count as 'doing the same kind of thing' in relation to that kind of activity ... Consider the parable of the Pharisee and the Publican ... Was the Pharisee who said

'God, I thank Thee that I am not as other men are' doing the same kind of thing as the Publican who prayed 'God be merciful unto me a sinner'? To answer this one would have to start by considering what is involved in the idea of prayer; and that is a *religious* question. In other words the appropriate criteria for deciding whether the actions of these two men were of the same kind or not belong to religion itself.[61]

This argument seems to me to rest on an undefended theory about the relation between rules of behaviour and criteria for identifying kinds of behaviour, namely that they must be the same, that the criteria for correctly describing some specimen of (rule-governed) behaviour, such as 'x-ing,' must be the same as the rules of x-ing. But why must the standards which are used to identify rule-governed activity be the same as the rules of that activity, that is, the standards that one engaging in the activity would endorse and seek to follow? Even if the proper scope of the social sciences is to be limited to study of these sorts of rules, why must the criteria for delimiting different sorts of subject matters be identical with the criteria embodied in the rules which (in Winch's view) make up those subject matters?

Winch might want to argue that a social scientist at least has to have had the experience of conventional rule following of some sort or other in order to understand the various rule-following activities of the subjects he studies, but this would make his view of what must be experienced by the social scientist similar to the third version of the *Verstehen* argument, which holds that the social scientist must at least know first hand what it is to act meaningfully. This obviously could not support anti-objectivist use of the limitations of the *Verstehen* argument, since all social scientists have had some experiences of meaningful activity – at least in the act of scientific investigation itself, which is purposive, has conventional rules of procedure, involves interpretation, and so on.

Verstehen The last version of what it is that the social scientist and his subject must have in common merits reflection. It suggests a way of regarding the whole *Verstehen* issue that might help to clarify the problems involved in analyzing it. In this third version the social scientist does not put himself imaginatively into the same sort of situation as the agent he wants to understand and then record how he himself would react. Nor does he try to relive the actor's probable experiences, or act in accord with the same rules. Rather he assumes that, just as his own actions are not merely blind reactions to stimuli, so the subject of his inquiry is likewise acting on some purposes or interpretations, and then the social scientist may or may not reflect on his own experience in trying to narrow down the scope of possible purposes. That is to say, the method of *Verstehen* is tied up with analogical reasoning. We interpret others' behaviour on the analogy of our own. This suggests that *Verstehen* analysis consists in explaining behaviour by means of a theory which includes reference to hypothesized mental states and events and employs the scientist's own mental activity as a model for the theoretical events and the states hypothesized.

Looked at in this way, various problems which have plagued the *Verstehen* dispute can be, if not solved, at least interpreted in ways which would bring the dispute into the mainstream of arguments in the philosophy of science. For instance, the dispute over whether *Verstehen* is a mere heuristic device, and what the mechanics (or structure) of *Verstehen* explanation are, might be absorbed into questions about the status of theoretical entities, the dispensability of models, and the mechanics of scientific model-construction and application, all of which have profited from extensive work in the philosophy of science.

The present dispute over the limitations of the possibility of objective study would be absorbed into such questions as how detailed the analogy between the model and the modelled must be in order for application to be fruitful, and whether the social scientist's own mental apparatus is the only possible model available. It might be argued that *Verstehen* so interpreted is not requisite even for an opponent of radical behaviourism, as long as it is possible, in principle at least, to explain behaviour by a theory using non-mental models for the hypothesized intervening variables. In this case the relative value of the *Verstehen* model would be contingent on its value in yielding elegant theoretical explanations, and helping to generate empirical hypotheses which are verified.

Historicism

The fourth kind of argument for anti-objectivism based on the fact that both the social scientist and his subject matter are humans is that, because of this fact, both he and his subjects are products of particular social circumstances, with particular conventions, habits of thought, and general perspectives.[62] To see the thrust of this consideration I believe it is necessary to return to the position of historicism. The argument which would give the consideration weight is one often raised in the sociology of knowledge. Social science, it is urged, reveals to us that all 'knowledge' is relative in that the methods for gaining it and the

criteria of sufficient evidence are determined by the special circumstances of a thinker's social environment, and these differ from historical period to historical period (or from social group to social group). But,
the argument continues, the social scientist is himself a human who lives
in a certain historical period and whose ideas and perspectives are
shaped by his relations with his contemporaries. Hence his own knowledge must also be relative. This position has already been examined in
chapter 1, but it will be instructive to come to it from a slightly different
direction here.

   The objectivist response to this argument is simply to deny that the
sociology of knowledge does or could support such a conclusion. Nagel
questions the empirical base of the argument. Maurice Mandelbaum
and Felix Kaufmann charge its advocates with confusing the psychological or social origins of a theory with the grounds for its justification.[63]
It was suggested in chapter 1 that the argument supposes an over-
simplified view of the history of scientific knowledge. Moreover the
argument is one of those which seem most clearly susceptible to
being self-defeating, or in greatest danger of falling into thoroughgoing
scepticism.[64]

THE 'NEW OBJECTIVITIES'

Against these charges social theorists have advanced several ways of
weakening the claim made by this argument, without giving up its basic
relativistic thrust. Since success in this attempt would at least limit what
could be objectively known, a brief survey of these attempts is in order.
In addition, these weakened forms of relativism are representative of
anti-objectivist social theorists' alternatives to an objectivist view of the
status of social-scientific inquiry, alternatives which purport to offer
what Karl Mannheim called 'a new type of objectivity.'[65]

   Typical representations of most of the views are to be found in
Mannheim's *Ideology and Utopia*. A good detailed exposition and
criticism of Mannheim's relativism is offered by Merton[66] (though the
criticisms are also applicable to some of Merton's own views[67]), and his
work will not be repeated here. But different candidates for the new
objectivity seem to me to have become part of the conventional wisdom
of social-scientific theory and deserve to be looked at in turn.

Pragmatism

One of the ways that Mannheim tries to limit his relativism is by espousing a kind of pragmatism: 'A theory ... is wrong if in a given practical situation it uses concepts and categories which, if taken seriously, would prevent man from adjusting himself at that historical stage.'[68] In addition to the considerations raised in chapter 3, a problem with this is that because of conflicts of interest, differences in abilities, etc., it is highly unlikely that at any stage there would be any *one* theory which would help everyone in a society to 'adjust.' So it would be necessary to discover just what the best interests of the society as a whole (presumably what Mannheim means by 'man' in the passage) are at that stage. But this would require social-scientific knowledge.

Control

Something like pragmatism is typically employed by Peter Berger and Thomas Luckmann as an undefended stipulative definition of 'reality' in their *The Social Construction of Reality*. For them 'reality' is defined as 'a quality appertaining to phenomena that we recognize as having a being independent of our own volition (we cannot "wish them away") ...'[69] The problem with this is that people cannot always 'wish away' delusions, despite the fact that beliefs based on them are easily seen by others to be false, and people can 'wish away' something by turning their backs on it or even destroying it (and then taking measures to repress memories of it).

Ideologies and utopias

Another argument is found in Mannheim's distinction between ideological and utopian ideals. A utopian theory is one which proves its own worth by producing the goals which it espouses:

Utopias ... transcend the social situation, for they ... orient conduct towards elements which the situation, in so far as it is realized at the time, does not contain. But they are not ideologies, i.e., they are not ideologies in the measure and in so far as they succeed through counter-activity in transforming the existing historical reality into one more in accord with their own conceptions.[70]

A problem with this view is that it is possible for people to act on the prescriptions of a theory and fail to bring about its embodied goals, or to act on one theory and to bring about the goals of another (possibly conflicting) theory. Therefore to sort 'true' from 'false' theories (utopias from ideologies) by this method would require determining which theories are acted on and whether it is the acting on those theories which has brought about the realization of their goals. But again this would require independent social-scientific knowledge.

Praxis

It is as a modification of the ideology-utopia argument that I think the relevant views of neo-Marxists who are in the tradition of Herbert Marcuse or who attempt to synthesize Marxism with phenomenology or existentialism are best seen. Philosophers like Jürgen Habermas employ the concept of '*Praxis*' (or of human 'projects' or of creative 'communicative action') to identify something analogous to Mannheim's utopias, but with some important differences.

Central to these theories is a differentiation between two kinds of thinking, one called, variously, 'technological,' 'instrumental,' or 'analytic,' the other, 'dialectical' or 'creative.' The first grows out of and also reinforces a kind of practice which inhibits free action and development of human potential; the other grows out of free, creative activity and helps to promote such activity. In neither case, in this view, do we discover some facts about man and society which exist independently of our values and beliefs, but rather in acting in certain ways a human and social reality is created (for instance, an action-stifling one or one where freedom predominates). If the practice is of the sort that promotes deterministic and pro-scientific attitudes, including belief in the possibility and desirablity of (the old) objectivity, it inhibits future creative practice, and these attitudes are to be rejected (much as Mannheim rejected 'ideologies') in favour of liberating practice-*cum*-attitudes which promote future creative practice.[71]

Without going into the web of specific philosophical views behind this appeal to *Praxis,* I think its inadequacies for producing a 'new objectivity' can be seen. It certainly cannot be denied that some actions do make important changes not only in our natural and social environments but also in our (normative and non-normative) attitudes. But it surely also cannot be denied that these actions take time and are complex; they are not just bursts of spontaneity or the like. Insofar as the anti-objectivists we are now discussing appeal to the name of Karl Marx, it seems not unfair to illustrate this point by considering the sort of practice that he and his followers actually engaged in, namely, revolutionary social practice; indeed this is all the more appropriate since, as Marxist thought (objectively pursued, in the old sense) shows, success in this action is what our society requires at this point in history. To help in bringing about the International Working Men's Association or the Bolshevik or Cuban revolutions men like Marx, Lenin, and Castro (among many others) had to organize meetings, write and distribute literature, form alliances, engage in military campaigns, and so on – all complex activities made up of many stages. And within these activities it surely made crucial differences to the final outcomes whether beliefs about the likely effects of doing one thing rather than another were objectively true (in the old sense).

A more general objection to the *Praxis* argument against (the old) objectivity is that it supposes that thinking scientifically (looking for laws, seeking objective truths in a controlled way, etc.) is incompatible with actions which develop human potential and liberate men. Suppose, as I think (against most proponents of the argument in question) Marx did,[72] that someone holds that a thorough scientific study of man itself shows that scientific thinking is the best, or the only, way to guide actions which can bring about liberation (where 'the free development of each is the condition for the free development of all'), what are advocates of this *Praxis* theory to say?

They cannot consistently challenge this conclusion by appealing to the very sort of (objectively pursued) inquiries they are concerned to denigrate, and the philosophical arguments they offer to show that scientifically based arguments in favour of the revolutionary advantages of scientific thinking cannot be correct seem to me to rest on one or more of the anti-objectivist views already discussed.[73] In fact, I think that if the relative correctness of the scientific arguments and of these philosophical counter-arguments are tested by their likely effects on revolutionary practices, the former will win, since a person who accepted the counter-arguments would not know what to do in a concrete situation and would be in danger of falling into a blind thrashing out or inactive despair.

'Progress'

Thomas Kuhn attempts to meet the charge that his theories lead to relativism in a way similar in some respects to pragmatism and the ideology-utopia view – by sketching a special notion of scientific progress (presumably both in the natural and social sciences). He holds that in regarding the evolutionary history of the sciences it 'should be easy,' by using criteria like 'accuracy of prediction,' 'number of difficult problems solved,' 'simplicity,' etc., to sort earlier from later theories and then to see that

... scientific development is, like biological, a unidirectional and irreversible process. Later scientific theories are better than earlier ones for solving puzzles in the often quite different environments to which they are applied. That is not a relativist's position, and it displays the sense in which I am a convinced believer in scientific progress.[74]

However it is evident that Kuhn, like Mannheim, requires (the old) objectivism in this argument. In order to determine where on the evolutionary scale a theory falls, one must know whether its predictions are accurate and how many difficult problems it actually does solve. And unless the question of whether a 'puzzle' has been solved is to be a mere matter of individual taste, some way of distinguishing failure and success in puzzle solving must be established. Kuhn rejects the obvious objectivist response to these difficulties on the grounds (similar to Mannheim's sceptical view that 'criteria of truth' vary historically) that there is 'no theory-independent way to reconstruct phrases like "really there," '[75] but he fails to offer any alternative to the objectivist position.

Relationism

Another of Mannheim's arguments for a new objectivity is associated by him with his doctrine of 'relationism.' He holds that the scientific suppositions of each age or in each social group can be taken as 'objectively true,' since a / they are true for those who share the suppositions, and b / the different systems of thought of different groups can be translated into one another's terms, and so objectively compared.[76] The first of these qualifications has already been examined in chapter 3. The other, as Nagel notes,[77] gives up relativism altogether and embraces objectivism.

Making suppositions explicit

A fourth way that Mannheim attempts to create a new objectivity is to advocate making the basic suppositions of an age explicit.[78] This is a very common argument of anti-objectivist social theorists, though it is seldom shown just why it should be thought to weaken the sceptical force of anti-objectivism. One would think that ignorance of the non-objectivity of their views is one of the few things that could save a social scientist from falling into sceptical despair.

One reason that Mannheim seems to think that this recognition will help create the new objectivity is that the social theorist will then be able to put his suppositions in the 'broader context' of other theories with *their* suppositions. Presumably there would be a kind of merging of theories into some sort of synthesis of views shared by most social scientists.[79] But it is hard to see how recognizing that there is a plurality of other suppositions (each non-objective) would lead theorists to effect such a merger (unless here too Mannheim is prepared to give up his historicistic relativism and urge that the point of comparison is to make objective choice).[80] The best this argument could lead to, I think, is the kind of neo-Kantian position, discussed in chapter 3, in which there is one set of suppositions for each cultural epoch.

Pluralism

Another reason Mannheim gives for the desirability of making suppositions explicit (possibly tied to his view of the enlightened 'intelligentsia') is that by this means 'free discussion' of them by social theorists is made possible.[81] But could there be any point in making such an examination if it were not to try to decide which of the various theories embodied in the suppositions was closest to the (objective) truth? Some philosophers have answered this question in the negative. For example, espousing a kind of philosophical liberalism which he calls 'pluralism,' P.K. Feyerabend argued at one point that a proliferation of rival theories is scientifically beneficial. It allows inquirers to borrow elements from one another's theories and from past theories, leaves many options open for a scientist if he should decide to abandon a theory, and inhibits dogmatism – the refusal seriously to entertain rival theories.[82]

On the face of it I see no reason why an objectivist (one adhering to the old type of objectivism) cannot agree. Surely scientists can and should be able to borrow from others' theories and entertain new theories, and surely dogmatism is a bad thing which scientists ought to combat by constantly reviewing their theories and examining the theories of others, always being prepared to alter or abandon their own theories in the light of these examinations. An objectivist can agree with this since in his view alteration or abandonment of theories could not be justified were it not possible for the examinations and reviews which prompt such action to be objective. Moreover, he should agree with anti-dogmatism, since it can be shown (objectively) that dogmatism inhibits the (objective) pursuit of science and the growth of knowledge.

However the objectivist agrees with the pluralist only on the surface. Behind the apparent agreement lies a difference about what the 'growth of knowledge' is. Feyerabend maintains:

Knowledge pluralistically conceived is not a process that converges toward an ideal view; it is an ever increasing ocean of alternatives, each of them forcing the others into greater articulation, all of them contributing, via this process of competion, to the development of our mental faculties.[83]

Here the virtue of having a plurality of theories is that this promotes the development of one's mental faculties. But this is a dubious view.

On the one hand, this kind of reasoning can be used, and often has been used, to defend the most rigorous dogmatism. From the alleged impossibility of even approximating to some (ideal) complete knowledge in any realm of inquiry, it may well be argued that therefore a person is best advised to take some one set of beliefs (religious or political beliefs, for example) and hold steadfastly to them so as to avoid being drowned in the ocean of alternatives. On the other hand, I think that it is probably a psychological truth that no matter how mentally stimulating entertaining a multitude of theories may be for certain periods of time, the long-range effects of refraining from adopting some theories and abandoning others would be to promote an eclectic habit of mind detrimental to creative thought and to deaden a person's mental faculties (not to mention the effect on his ability to act on the basis of scientific conclusions).

Common sense

Another argument that the suppositions should be made explicit is to be found in Cicourel's book.[84] He argues that the most basic presuppositions of a social scientist, the common sense theories embedded in his everyday language, are bound to be those also of the members of his society. So if the scientist makes these presuppositions explicit, then he can make the shared common sense theory the basis of his general social theory. Thus his social theory would so to speak 'match' his subject matter. This argument (advanced by Cicourel, appropriately or not, in support of Parsonian action theory) requires that there are presupposed theories common to all members of a society. Cicourel avoids the problem of presupposing (the old) objectivity which would be involved in a defence of his view by means of social-scientific inquiry by appealing instead to the work of some philosophers of language, but only at the cost of confronting the problems of linguistic relativism discussed in chapter 3. In addition, this version of a new objectivism amounts to the essentially sceptical view already discussed that objectivity is possible only within certain frameworks of presupposition, since there are (at least the possibilities of) differences in the common sense theories of different societies, and therefore, in Cicourel's view, in the 'objective' theories of their social scientists.

Intersubjectivity

Just the same considerations apply to a view sometimes derived from the theories of phenomenologists. It is said that an examination of common sense 'experience' (including people's belief formations) with an eye to uncovering its 'presuppositions' shows, among other things, that one's beliefs are formed in social interaction and crucially involve beliefs about others' (actual or possible) beliefs in such a way that the social scientist is justified (even *bound* in some way) to accept those theories which are in accord with the presuppositions of intersubjectively formed and sustained common sense beliefs, which, of course, he and his subjects share.[85] Possibly it could then be said that this criterion of justification replaces one appealing to objectivity in the 'old' sense. Thus in one of his attempts to solve the problem of historicism Maurice Merleau-Ponty links the concept of 'intersubjectivity' with what he calls 'a new idea of truth.'[86]

But the same problems arise, viz., of avoiding presupposing the old objectivity if the examination of common sense on which this theory is based is empirical, or of avoiding scepticism and the specific difficulties of anti-objectivist arguments discussed in chapters 2 through 4 above, if it is philosophical. In addition, there is a special problem should an examination of people's (common sense) beliefs about the rational adequacy of beliefs show (as I think it does) that within common sense the 'old' objectivity is supposed, a conclusion, interestingly, that the best known phenomenologically oriented philosopher of social science, Alfred Schutz, seems himself to have come to.[87]

The new 'objectivists' all face a similar problem. They all suppose some view of man and society which needs to be defended by them. Philosophical defences involve one or more of the anti-objectivist positions we have been examining. Defences which involve social-scientific investigation confront the new objectivist with a kind of dilemma. He might say that this investigation can be carried out objectively, in the 'old' sense, which is to give up any pretense of being a critic of objectivism. Or he might admit that it is *impossible* to avoid circular reasoning or a regress in any such defence, and then the new objectivity turns into the old anti-objectivism.

CHAPTER SIX

Postscript on the morality of objectivity

An argument perhaps once more popular among scholars than today, but still heard in different forms as part of conventional wisdom, is that the pursuit of social-scientific inquiry with the intent to discover truths about one's social reality has morally undesirable consequences.[1] In the case of some of these arguments it is precisely the pursuit of objectivity which is criticized; while in most it is simply the pursuing of social-scientific inquiry itself (whether objectively or not) which is thought to be objectionable. In the latter case I think that the possibility of objectivity in social science is supposed, since it is this possibility that makes for the effectiveness of social science in describing and predicting human behaviour, and since it is the quest for objectivity (at least believed to be possible by social scientists) that prompts developing the social-scientific techniques to which some critics object.

The question of whether or not objective social-scientific inquiry is morally objectionable is no doubt not seen as a major problem by most social scientists. They would, I believe, agree with the following comment of W.H. Werkmeister:

The question of value *of* the social sciences constitutes no particular problem. Insofar as any knowledge in whatever field of inquiry is of value to us, the knowledge obtained in the social sciences is, of course, also of value. ... On the one hand, knowledge is valued simply for its own sake, as satisfying man's innate curiosity. ... On the other hand, however, it is also a fact that knowledge is of crucial importance as the basis for rational decisions and reasonable actions, that it has practical or pragmatic value in the service of man's aspirations, intentions, and hopes – including his aspiration to understand himself and to control his environment.[2]

Surely the view expressed here is correct. How can cures for social ills be found unless the nature of the society is known, and how can decisions about what course of social action to take be rationally made without knowing what the likely consequences of various courses of action would be?

Nonetheless the moral undesirability of social-scientific pursuits is urged, and looking at some of the grounds for this sentiment is perhaps a suitable conclusion to the present endeavour. I think of four kinds of grounds, sometimes stated and often implied, in morally motivated attacks on social science: that social science can be put to immoral purposes, that it dehumanizes, that it promotes an attitude of detachment, and that it may reach undesirable conclusions.

The use of social science

The first of these does not seem to me to withstand much examination. This is the view, similar to one urged against all science, that social-scientific knowledge is a potentially dangerous tool – in the hands of propagandists for instance. Social scientists themselves have recognized the unhappy fact that the social-scientific tool is often put to immoral use. But what is at issue is whether or not such uses are inevitable (or at least not minimizable) and whether the danger of such misuse outweighs the social good which can be brought about by social science.[3]

It is at least doubtful that the social sciences have brought about more ill than good, and in any case social science would have to be used to find this out (and the task would probably be so great as to require maintaining and cultivating most of the techniques and attitudes that critics see as potentially morally dangerous anyway). In addition, this sort of criticism faces the rejoinder often given to moral critics of natural sciences, that the very potency of the social-scientific tool requires that social science be pursued by those who would not put it to immoral uses in order successfully to combat those who would. For example, propaganda is best resisted by an educated and informed populace, but developing effective educational techniques and modes of disseminating information requires social-scientific work.

Dehumanization

Arguments that the social sciences dehumanize can be divided into two groups.[4] Some critics seem to think that the pursuing of social science dehumanizes the social scientist; it causes him to regard his fellow men clinically or experimentally as mere objects. In one respect this is probably true. The social scientist, like the doctor, thinks of people differently in his professional and non-professional capacities in that as a social scientist he is interested in their actions and beliefs for the special purposes of scientific explanation and description. But, as was argued in chapter 5, there is no reason to think that taking up such an attitude prevents the social scientist from taking up other attitudes in his day-to-day interactions any more than the doctor is hampered in this way. Indeed the knowledge gained while taking the scientific attitude could even help the social scientist in his non-professional capacity by making him aware of inobvious pressures on people and hence more tolerant of their shortcomings.

Another view is that social-scientific study in a community dehumanizes the members of that community. Sometimes the possibility of social manipulation is cited as an instance of the dehumanizing effect,[5] but not all social 'manipulation' (a more neutral word would perhaps be 'planning') works against the dignity and freedom of the individual (for instance, if it is carried on with his knowledge and consent for the sake of bettering living conditions and opening the possibilities for development). So this argument is a species of the last.

At other times it is held that social science leads the people studied to think of themselves as not free, or mere objects, in a way appropriate for the scientist but not for the socially interacting individual. A view like this is advanced by those of an existentialist bent who consider such a scientific attitude a form of bad faith, and one critic of the social sciences sees it as typical of the spread of a 'scientistic' temper:

Along with the acceptance of these denials [of 'subjective experience'] comes the habit of looking upon man as we look upon the other animals, simultaneously failing to realize the consequences of our change of attitude. But we cannot maintain our self-respect if implicit in our approach to ourselves and others lies the conviction that man is only that which science says he is. And one of the consequences of a loss of self-respect is that the fiber of actual living is coarsened.[6]

One thing that those who criticize acting or thinking in bad faith mean by this is acting or thinking in a way which is not in accord with one's true nature. So if the critic of social-scientific thought argues on these grounds, it must be because he thinks it is not in accord with one's true nature. This argument obviously supposes either anti-objectivism or the fact that the extant social sciences come to (objectively) false conclusions; the first position has been the topic of this book, and the second is best proven (and remedied), I maintain, by the use of social-scientific thought to come to (objectively) *true* conclusions.

The basic thrust of this dehumanization argument, however, is that once people begin to think of themselves as possible objects of social-scientific knowledge, action and the quest for discovery will be inhibited. The fact that at different times social scientists have been among the leaders of the struggle for social changes should be *prima facie* evidence against this argument. Also the point about self-respect works two ways. While it may be that social-scientific study reveals that men are more like other animals than like angels, it surely also can provide good, objective reasons (as opposed to superstitions) for believing that humans are in several ways qualitatively different from the other animals, thus placing attitudes of human self-respect on firmer ground than before the development of social-scientific thought.

What I think often lies behind these dehumanization arguments is a certain philosophical attitude toward determinism which ought at least to be mentioned. It is thought that, if people regard themselves scientifically, they will believe their thoughts and actions to be causally determined, and lapse into inactivity. The topic of determinism is philosophically complex, but suffice it here to note that this attitude identifies the doctrine of universal causal determinism with the doctrine of fatalism, i.e., the view that human thoughts and values can themselves play no causal roles in the history of individuals and societies. But this identification needs to be defended.[7] Indeed it is precisely the humanistic potential of social-scientific thought that (if objectively carried out) enables it to play an important causal role in bettering the human condition by promoting free human action (in discovering the impediments to such action and making predictions about ways of removing them).

Detachment

Many of the arguments so far discussed were most forcefully put forth in the 1930s and 40s, more often than not advanced by theorists of the right and directed against social scientists who were at that time engaged in activities of social reform and revolution. In North America today, however, it seems to me that there is a larger proportion of social scientists (at least in universities) who, far from being involved in socially progressive action, take a position quite aloof from such action or even attempt to show that this activity is futile and misguided, all in the name of objectivity. This has prompted criticisms of the morality of objectivity for promoting an attitude of detachment in those social scientists who do favour social activism. Indeed one recent critic of 'establishment' sociology, Alvin Gouldner, seems to use 'objectivity' and 'detachment' as synonyms.[8]

But if some social scientists who in practice defend the status quo advance the view that objectivity and social activism are incompatible, I do not see why the activist should share their view. Sometimes this criticism of objectivity is based on the *Praxis* arguments discussed in the last chapter, and suffers from the problems noted there. As it stands, as good a case (in my opinion a decisively better case) can be made out for the opposite of the detachment argument. Insofar as social-scientific work shows that it is possible (not to say desirable[9]) to change things for the better, it encourages people to try bringing changes about by means of social action.

Moral anarchy

The view that the findings of the social sciences may have undesirable moral consequences is most frequently seen in the fear that the social sciences will unseat traditional values, thereby producing social chaos.[10] A person holding this view may say that if social-scientific work converts people to moral relativism or to a thesis like Robert Ardrey's – that men are essentially amoral, predatory beasts – then the action in accord with moral standards necessary for the functioning of society would cease. Whether social sciences like sociology and anthropology actually do support either of these views is a position with empirical and (in the case of moral relativism) philosophical bases not nearly as easily established as is sometimes thought by those who advance them.[11] However it is usually argued that, whether these views are true or not, their acceptance can have socially disintegrative effects.

Now what is at issue here is an empirical question regarding the effects of social science. While it may be true that students of social science sometimes change some of their values, this does not count as evidence for the view in question. This view is that as a matter of fact such students are likely to cease being moral agents at all. The existence of social scientists and their students who remain moral agents even if they claim to embrace the Ardrey thesis or to hold to moral relativism is *prima facie* evidence that a thorough empirical study may not support this conclusion. Surely the mere possibility that such a study might support the conclusion is slim grounds for condemning the social-scientific enterprise, and would certainly not justify abandoning it.

Were a study tending to support such unhappy conclusions actually carried out, then (philosophical problems aside) the moral debate would, no doubt, take on not a little importance. But for social theorists, philosophers of social science, and various guardians of the public morality to take such debate seriously, the study had better be objective!

NOTES

CHAPTER ONE

1 F.A. Hayek, *The Counter-Revolution of Science* (Glencoe, 1955), part I, chaps. 2, 3.
Talcott Parsons, *The Structure of Social Action* (Glencoe, 1949), see pp. 46, 348–9.
Stephen Strasser, *Phenomenology and the Human Sciences* (Pittsburgh, 1963), passim; Strasser sometimes also offers a definition of 'objective' in terms of a 'feeling of constraint' men have in recognizing that some things cannot be controlled at will (pp. 85–6), but in other places Strasser uses 'objective' in a sense (compatible with this psychological one) which is more like that employed in the present work (pp. 203–4).
Ludwig von Mises, *Theory and History* (London, 1958), chap. XI.

2 Max Weber, *The Theory of Social and Economic Organization,* trans. A.M. Henderson and Talcott Parsons (Glencoe, 1964), pp. 87–115. I see no reason why a Weberian subjectivist cannot also be an objectivist. On the other hand, while Weber is often cited as a defender of objectivism in his debates about '*Wertfreiheit,*' for the most part I believe he advances arguments favouring anti-objectism, allowing for 'objectivity' only in one of the 'new' forms criticized in chap. 5 below.

3 A point overlooked by Ernest Nagel in his otherwise excellent criticism of Weber in *The Structure of Science* (New York, 1961), pp. 485ff.

4 See Aristotle, *Metaphysics,* book IV, chap. 7: 'To say of what is that it is not, or of what is not that it is, is false, while to say of what is that it is, and of what is not that it is not, is true.'

5 There are philosophical debates over what is to count as 'justification,' but in the present work it will suffice simply to employ my colleague D. Goldstick's concept of 'epistemically justified': '... for a belief to be "epistemically justified" means that in the interests of truth it is best to hold it (in the existing circumstances); a belief will thus be "epistemically justified" only if it is not an *error* (note that in the sense which is relevant here a true belief can be held *in error* and a false belief can be held *without error* – for example,

it is sometimes only by *erring* medically that a doctor hits upon that diagnosis which happens to be factually correct in the instance at hand). If a *belief* is to the *truth* the way a shot at a given target is to the target shot at, then a *justified belief*, in this analogy, simply means one which is, as it were "shot well." ' In 'Methodological Conservatism,' *American Philosophical Quarterly*, VIII, 2 (April 1971), 186–91.

6 R.M.MacIver, *Society* (New York, 1931), p. 529.
   von Mises, *Theory and History*.

7 The scientific problems for an infinity-of-nature view are similar to those discussed by Florian Znaniecki as the problems of the 'circumscription of systems' of objects of study, in *The Method of Sociology* (New York, 1934), pp. 8–16. But Znaniecki sees no problem for objectivity here.

8 As is supposed by William Earl, 'The Standard Observer in the Sciences of Man,' *Ethics*, LXIII, 4 (July 1953), 293–9, esp. pp. 295–7.
   And MacIver, *Society,* p. 530.

9 This supposition is to be found in Isaiah Berlin's *Historical Inevitability* (London, 1954), pp. 18ff; and in Benedetto Croce, 'Historical Determinism and the "Philosophy of History," ' in Patrick Gardiner, ed., *Theories of History* (New York, 1959), pp. 233–41, originally publ. in *History – Its Theory and Practice,* trans. E.T. Carritt (London, 1949), chap. 4. In these works Berlin and Croce usually mean to include all the 'cultural sciences' in their attacks on 'naturalistic' views of history.

10 Aaron V. Cicourel, *Method and Measurement in Sociology* (Glencoe, 1964), passim.
   Michael Polanyi, *Science, Faith, and Society* (Chicago, 1946), pp. 28ff.

11 Abraham Kaplan, *The Conduct of Inquiry* (San Francisco, 1964), pp. 371ff.
   Harold D. Lasswell, 'Strategies of Inquiry,' in Daniel Lerner, ed., *The Human Meaning of the Social Sciences* (Cleveland, 1959), pp. 89–113.
   Gunnar Myrdal, *Objectivity in Social Research* (New York, 1969), passim.
   Michael Polanyi, *Personal Knowledge* (London, 1958), p. 135.

12 Max Weber, *The Methodology of the Social Sciences,* trans. Edward Shils and Henry Finch (New York, 1949), p. 76, and see pp. 80–1.

13 See Kaplan, *Conduct of Inquiry,* pp. 381–2, who later violates his own criticism.

14 Gunnar Myrdal, *Value in Social Theory* (London, 1958), pp. 1, 154.

15 Myrdal, *Objectivity in Social Research,* pp. 43, 47, 51, 55–6. An example of a passage in this work which implies anti-objectivism is: 'But I do insist that if we place ourselves under the obligation to spell out, in as definite terms as possible, a set of instrumental value premises ... and if we allow them to *determine* our approach, the definitions of our concepts, and the formulation of our theories, this represents an advance towards the goals of honesty, clar-

ity, and effectiveness in research. These are steps in the direction of "objectivity" in the only sense this concept can be understood' (p. 72, italics added). The sense in which these values 'determine' the approach, etc., is not spelled out by Myrdal. For criticism of the implied views expressed here see the sections on 'Objectivism and Anti-Objectivism' and 'The New Objectivities' in chaps. 1 and 5 of this book.

16 James Leach, 'Explanation and Value Neutrality,' *British Journal for the Philosophy of Science,* XIX, 2 (Aug. 1968), 93–108; Polanyi, *Science, Faith, and Society,* pp. 67–82.
Nagel, *Structure of Science,* pp. 497–8.

17 David Bohm, *Causality and Chance in Modern Physics* (New York, 1957), chap. 1. Here Bohm argues this point for the most difficult case, that of quantum mechanics, where the most forceful arguments have been presented to show that randomness is an essential feature of a scientific subject matter, so that *only* probabilistic laws would be possible – even in principle.

18 Leo Strauss, quoted in Nagel, *Structure of Science,* p. 490.

19 Nagel, *Structure of Science,* p. 493.

20 R.G. Collingwood, *The Idea of History* (New York, 1956), chap. 5, esp. pp. 214–18.

21 Berlin, *Historical Inevitability,* p. 53.

22 William Dray, *Laws and Explanation in History* (London, 1957), p. 124.

23 William Dray, 'Some Causal Accounts of the American Civil War,' *Daedalus,* XCI (Summer 1960), 578–92; the pertinent section of this article is reprinted in his *Philosophy of History* (Englewood Cliffs, 1964), pp. 47–57. An even tighter connection between explanations of actions and appraisal is urged by H.L.A. Hart, 'The Ascription of Responsibility and Rights,' *Proceedings of the Aristotelian Society,* n.s. XLIX (1948), 171–94, who argues that the 'principal function' of 'sentences of the form "He did it" ' is not to describe an action but 'to ascribe responsibility for actions'; alone, however, this view would not support anti-objectivism, since objective determination of the characteristics which spark ascriptions of responsibility (those characteristics the descriptions of which Hart claims are incorrectly considered primary in action explanations) would still be possible; moreover Hart's claim that the ascriptive function of such language is primary is not without philosophical problems.
See George Pitcher, 'Hart on Action and Responsibility,' *Philosophical Review,* LXIX (April 1960), 226–35.
Also see James Rachels, 'On Liking,' *Analysis,* XXIX, 4 (Mar. 1969), 143–4.

24 See Myrdal, *Value in Social Theory,* passim, esp. pp. 1ff, 154–5; and Berlin, *Historical Inevitability.*

25 See S.F. Nadel, *The Foundations of Social Anthropology* (London, 1951), pp. 53–4, and Quentin Gibson, *The Logic of Social Enquiry* (London, 1960),

pp. 63–4; such a confusion seems to me to lie behind the views of both these theorists, though the first is an anti-objectivist and the latter an objectivist; for a criticism, see Richard Rudner, *Philosophy of Social Science* (Englewood Cliffs, 1966), p. 86.

Myrdal, *Objectivity in Social Research,* pp. 15, 57–8.

26 Dray, *Laws and Explanations in History,* pp. 28–9.

Collingwood, *Idea of History,* p. 215.

Also see W.H. Walsh, *Philosophy of History: An Introduction* (London, 1967), p. 97.

And Wilhelm Windelband, *An Introduction to Philosophy,* trans. J.H. Tufts (London, 1921), who writes: 'An event becomes historical when, in virtue of its individual significance, it is directly or indirectly related to values. Thus the empirical science of history creates its objects, since it gives prominence amongst the immense variety of events to those which may be of interest on account of their relations to value, and it then combines the separate elements in constructions which in turn are related to values' (pp. 278–9).

27 Karl Mannheim, *Ideology and Utopia* (New York, 1936), p. 271.

28 Ibid., pp. 82–3.

29 Ibid., p. 288.

30 Ibid., pp. 290–2.

31 Ibid., see pp. 74–5, 276–7; one of Mannheim's reservations about Marxism seems to be that it inconsistently applies an historicist argument only to views held by those whom it opposes (p. 139). Marx, however, neither exempted his own views from historical-social conditioning, nor, for the reason given below, did he need to in order consistently to advance them as objective.

32 Karl Marx, *On Malthus,* trans. Dorthea Meek and Ronald Meek (New York, 1954), p. 120.

33 Karl Marx, *Capital,* I, preface to 2nd English ed. (Moscow, 1954), p. 14.

34 V.I. Lenin, *Materialism and Empirio-Criticism* (Moscow, 1964), p. 123.

35 Myrdal, *Value in Social Theory,* p. 153.

36 Weber, *Methodology of the Social Sciences,* pp. 72–3, 111.

37 Polanyi, *Science, Faith, and Society,* pp. 21–2.

38 Cicourel, *Method and Measurement,* pp. 21–2 and passim.

Hayek, *Counter-Revolution of Science,* pp. 47ff.

39 Polanyi, *Personal Knowledge,* p. 161.

Michael Polanyi, *The Tacit Dimension* (London, 1967), p. 64.

40 Kaplan, *Conduct of Inquiry,* p. 386.

41 Mannheim, *Ideology and Utopia,* p. 271.

42 Cicourel, *Method and Measurement,* p. 24.

P.K. Feyerabend, 'Explanation, Reduction, and Empiricism,' in Herbert Feigl and Grover Maxwell, eds., *Minnesota Studies in the Philosophy of Sci-*

ence (Minneapolis, 1962), III, 29.

Thomas S. Kuhn, *The Structure of Scientific Revolutions* (Chicago, 1962), p. 110.

Stephen Toulmin, *Foresight and Understanding* (Bloomington, 1961), pp. 95–6.

43 Possibly such an argument is in the background of (the late) N.R. Hanson's chap. 'Facts' in his *Patterns of Discovery* (Cambridge, 1958), pp. 31–49, hence explaining the uncharacteristic lack of argumentation for the antiobjectivist position presented in that chap.

44 Israel Scheffler, *Science and Subjectivity* (Indianapolis, 1967).

Richard Rudner, 'The Scientist Qua Scientist Makes Value Judgments,' in L.I. Krimerman, ed., *The Nature and Scope of Social Science* (New York, 1969), pp. 754–8, originally publ. in *Philosophy of Science,* XX, 20 (Jan. 1953), 1–6; the comments made about views attributed to W.V.O. Quine in chap. 3 of this book will apply equally to Rudner's defence of the arguments from value.

45 Peter Alexander, *Sensationalism and Scientific Explanation* (London, 1963), p. 92.

Robert E. Butts, 'Feyerabend and the Pragmatic Theory of Observation,' *Philosophy of Science,* XXXIII, 4 (Dec. 1966), 382 – 94.

Gibson, *Logic of Social Enquiry,* p. 86.

Nagel, *Structure of Science,* pp. 500–1.

Scheffler, *Science and Subjectivity,* pp. 13ff.

Dudley Shapere, 'Meaning and Scientific Change,' in Robert G. Colodny, ed., *Mind and Cosmos* (Pittsburgh, 1966), pp. 57, 65.

CHAPTER TWO

1 Mary Hesse, 'Theories, Dictionaries, and Observation,' *British Journal for the Philosophy of Science* [hereafter cited as BJPS], IX, 33 (May 1958), 12–28.

2 Peter Alexander, 'Theory Construction and Theory Testing,' BJPS, IX, 33 (May 1958), 29–38.

3 P.K. Feyerabend, 'Explanation, Reduction, and Empiricism,' in Herbert Feigl and Grover Maxwell, eds., *Minnesota Studies in the Philosophy of Science* (Minneapolis, 1962), III, 28–97.

4 Ibid., p. 29.

5 Ibid., p. 43.

6 Ibid., p. 48, italics omitted; see also pp. 45, 47, 49, 59.

7 Ibid., p. 57, italics omitted.

8 Gustav Bergmann, 'Imperfect Knowledge,' in May Brodbeck, ed., *Readings in the Philosophy of the Social Sciences* (New York, 1968), pp. 415–35, originally publ. in *Philosophy of Science* (Madison, 1957), pp. 115–24.

May Brodbeck, 'Explanation, Prediction and ''Imperfect'' Knowledge,' in

Herbert Feigl and Grover Maxwell, eds., *Minnesota Studies in the Philosophy of Science* (Minneapolis, 1962), III, 363–97.

9 See the insightful criticism of Feyerabend's view of scientific progress by Dudley Shapere, 'Meaning and Scientific Change,' in Robert G. Colodny, ed., *Mind and Cosmos* (Pittsburgh, 1966), pp. 41–85.

10 An example of this confusion can be seen in Feyerabend's criticism of the defence made by Hempel and others of their view of the relations among competing theories. It is sometimes held against Feyerabend's criticisms of the possibility of the (logical) reduction of theories like Galileo's to those like Newton's – that is, the (deductive) explanation of the laws of the former by means of the laws of the latter – that in such cases what are explained are not the laws of, e.g., Galileo, but corrected versions of his laws; see Carl Hempel, *Aspects of Scientific Explanation* (New York, 1965), p. 344.

Feyerabend's criticism is that this is an 'admission of defeat' on the part of deductivists; see P.K. Feyerabend, 'Reply to Criticism,' in Robert S. Cohen and Marx W. Wartofsky, eds., *Boston Studies in the Philosophy of Science* (Boston, 1965), II, 223–61, esp. p. 229.

But in what sense is it a defeat? Feyerabend is arguing that such a move does not allow the deductivists to explain the relationships among *actual* competing theories in the history of science; and, from the point of view of the actual grounds on which one theory is accepted over another, this may have some force. But, for our purposes, the deductivist argument need not be seen as one about the grounds on which scientific theories are justifiably accepted or abandoned; rather it is one about what it means to explain in science. Thus it is important for the deductivist to give meaning to such phrases as 'approximate explanation' or 'partial explanation,' and it seems quite legitimate to introduce hypothetical intermediate theories, such as the corrected version of Galileo's, for this purpose.

For another, related criticism of Feyerabend on the same point see Hempel, *Aspects of Scientific Explanation,* p. 347, n17.

Also see J.J.C. Smart, *Between Science and Philosophy* (New York, 1968), pp. 86–7.

While I think it is a mistake to regard the deductive-nomological model of explanation as a theory about what constitutes scientific evidence, Hempel no doubt does presuppose part of an answer to this question when he cites in favour of the deductivist model its ability to 'clearly satisfy what is, I submit, a general *condition of adequacy* for any account that is to qualify as a rationally acceptable explanation of a given event. The condition is that any such explanation, i.e., any rationally acceptable answer to a question of the type "Why did X occur?" must provide information which constitutes good grounds for the belief that X did in fact occur' (in Sidney Hook, ed., *Philosophy and History,* New York, 1963, p. 146). What Hempel presupposed in saying this, so far as deductive-nomological explanation is concerned, was that, in the case of a valid deductive explanation of the occurrence of an event X, the information contained in statements of initial conditions and laws, if accepted, constitutes good grounds for the belief that X did in fact occur. It would surely take a more extreme anti-objectivist than any who are actually in contention to deny this.

11 Thomas S. Kuhn, *The Structure of Scientific Revolutions,* 1st ed. (Chicago, 1962), p. 10.

12 Ibid., p. 93.

13 Stephen Toulmin, *Foresight and Understanding* (Bloomington, 1961), p. 95.

14 S.F. Nadel, *The Foundations of Social Anthropology* (London, 1951), p. 49.

15 Israel Scheffler, *Science and Subjectivity* (Indianapolis, 1967), p. 15.
Shapere, 'Meaning and Scientific Change,' pp. 52ff.

16 See Max Weber, *The Methodology of the Social Sciences,* trans. Edward Shils and Henry Finch (New York, 1949), p. 84.

17 See Scheffler, *Science and Subjectivity,* pp. 80–1.

18 See Kuhn, *Scientific Revolutions,* p. 102.

19 Ibid., pp. 108–9.

20 Ibid., p. 109.

21 Ibid., pp. 10–11.

22 Thomas S. Kuhn, *The Structure of Scientific Revolutions,* 2nd ed., enlarged, *International Encyclopedia of Unified Science,* II, 2 (Chicago, 1970), pp. 189–90.

This seems to be the way R.W. Friedrichs interprets paradigms in his application of Kuhn's theory to the history of sociology, *A Sociology of Sociology* (New York, 1970), p. 4, interpreting this to mean that paradigms provide 'a fundamental image of the nature of one's subject matter,' p. 36. Friedrich lists three main sociological paradigms – the 'system image' of functionalism, 'conflict paradigms' of conflict theory, and the 'dialectical frame' of Marxism and neo-Marxism – and says that the latter two grew to challenge functionalism due to its failure to accommodate the 'anomaly' of social change, pp. 25ff. For this to illustrate a paradigm shift in the way required by anti-objectivism it would have to be shown that conflict theorists and Marxists could not have been objective in abandoning functionalism. Yet even on Friedrich's account of the history of sociological theory it looks as if functionalism was challenged simply on the grounds that it could not produce an (objectively) adequate account of the important feature of human societies that they change.

23 Ibid., pp. 192, 194, 200–1.

24 In this postscript Kuhn denies that he is a 'relativist' or a glorifier of 'irrationality,' using the terms in ways that would probably include anti-objectivism and scepticism. One of the grounds for this denial will be

examined in chapters 3 and 5 of this book. Another is discussed in connection with Kuhn's treatment of 'shared values.' Kuhn argues that there can be variability in the application of shared values and that having shared values plays an important parts both in the progress of normal science and in scientific revolutions (p. 186). However this does not rescue him from the charge of advocating anti-objectivism, since these values seem to be ones shared by scientists employing the *same* paradigms; while what is at issue in the objectivist – anti-objectivist debate is whether objective choice *among* paradigms is possible.

25 Michael Polanyi, *Personal Knowledge* (London, 1958), pp. 299ff, 251.
Michael Polanyi, *Science, Faith, and Society* (Chicago, 1946), pp. 54–5, 70–3.
Michael Polanyi, *The Tacit Dimension* (London, 1967), pp. 69–70, 77–8.

26 Kuhn, *Scientific Revolutions*, p. 77.

27 Herbert Butterfield, *The Origins of Modern Science* (New York, 1962), p. 13 (first publ. 1949).

28 Scheffler, *Science and Subjectivity*, p. 74.

29 Polanyi, *Science, Faith, and Society*, chap. 2.

30 Kuhn, *Scientific Revolutions*, pp. 8–9.

31 Scheffler, *Science and Subjectivity*, pp. 69ff.

32 Hans Reichenbach, *Experience and Prediction* (Chicago, 1938), pp. 5–7.

33 Polanyi, *Personal Knowledge*, pp. 134, 135, 143.
See Carl Hempel, *Philosophy of Natural Science* (Englewood Cliffs, 1966), pp. 15ff.

34 Michael Scriven, 'Insight and Understanding,' *Proceedings of the Seventh Inter-American Congress of Philosophy*, University of Laval (Quebec, 1967), pp. 20–35.

35 It is this point which prompts Gibson's criticism of the use of the discovery-justification distinction; Quentin Gibson, *The Logic of Social Enquiry* (London, 1960), p. 75.

36 Butterfield, *Origins of Modern Science*, p. 17.

37 Stephen F. Mason, *A History of the Sciences* (New York, 1962), p. 119.

38 Butterfield, *Origins of Modern Science*, p. 24.

39 See, for instance, Polanyi, *Science, Faith, and Society*, pp. 90ff.

40 Butterfield, *Origins of Modern Science*, pp. 1, 155ff.
Kuhn, *Scientific Revolutions*, pp. 52–6.
E.A. Burtt, *The Metaphysical Foundations of Modern Physical Science* (New York, 1932), pp. 165–7.

41 Kuhn, *Scientific Revolutions*, chap. 10, especially pp. 121ff.

42 Polanyi, *Science, Faith, and Society*, pp. 28 and 31 respectively; see also, *Personal Knowledge*, p. 157.

43 Wilfrid Sellars, 'The Language of Theories,' in Herbert Feigl and Grover

Maxwell, eds., *Current Issues in the Philosophy of Science* (New York, 1960), p. 22.

See Ernest Nagel, *The Structure of Science* (New York, 1961), chap. 5.

Hempel, *Philosophy of Natural Science,* pp. 70ff.

R.B. Braithwaite, *Scientific Explanation* (New York, 1960), p. 22.

CHAPTER THREE

1 Aaron V. Cicourel, *Method and Measurement in Sociology* (Glencoe, 1964), p. 1.

See also Robert K. Merton, *Social Theory and Social Structure* (Glencoe, 1964), pp. 91–2.

2 Benjamin Lee Whorf, in John B. Carroll, ed., *Language, Thought, and Reality* (Cambridge, Mass., 1964), p. 214.

Eduard Sapir, in David G. Mandelbaum, ed., *Sellected Writings of Eduard Sapir in Language, Culture and Personality* (Berkeley, 1949), p. 162.

3 For a summary of Humboldtian linguistic relativism see Harold Basilius, 'Neo-Humboldtian Ethnolinguistics,' *Word,* xxii, 2 (June 1965), 207–20.

For Cassirer see Ernst Cassirer, *Language and Myth* (New York, 1946), p. 9 and chap. 3, esp. pp. 24–5, 28.

4 Whorf, *Language,* passim; see esp. pp. 55, 58ff, 104–5, 137, 147ff, 152–3, 156, 214, 221, 239, 252.

5 Ibid., p. 221.

Sapir, 'Conceptual Categories in Primitive Language,' a paper read at the National Academy of Sciences, New Haven, November 1931, summarized in *Science,* lxxiv, no. 1927 (Dec. 1931), 578.

6 Roger Brown, *Words and Things* (Glencoe, 1958), esp. chaps. 6, 7.

Eric H. Lenneberg, 'Cognition in Ethnolinguistics,' *Language,* xxix, 4 (Oct. 1953), 463–71.

Marjorie Pyles, 'Verbalization as a Factor in Learning,' *Child Development,* iii, 2 (June 1932), 108–13.

7 See, for example, Franz Boas, 'Language and Culture,' in *Studies in the History of Culture* (Madison, 1942), who concludes on the basis of his studies that: 'I think our general experience in the field of linguistic data proves that language is a reflex of culture and that there are everywhere linguistic devices that enable the language to follow the demands of culture' (p. 181), and that 'culture controls the growth of language; the opposite influence is slight' (p. 183).

8 Whorf, *Language,* pp. 79–80.

Sapir, *Writings,* pp. 160–6.

9 See Max Black, 'Linguistic Relativism: the Views of Benjamin Lee Whorf,'

in *Models and Metaphors* (Ithaca, 1962), pp. 244–57, originally publ. in *The Philosophical Review,* LXVIII, 2 (Apr. 1959), 228–38.

10 Whorf, *Language,* pp. 143–7, 155, 216, 269.

11 Ibid., p. 140.

12 Paul Radin, *Primitive Religion* (New York, 1957).
Mircea Eliade, *Cosmos and History* (New York, 1954), see esp. the foreword: 'We hold that philosophical anthropology would have something to learn from the valorization that pre-Socratic man (in other words, traditional man) accorded to his situation in the universe' (p. xii).

13 Whorf, *Language,* pp. 135–7.

14 Ibid., p. 216.
For a criticism see C.A. Brutyan, 'The Philosophical Bearings of the Theory of Linguistic Relativity,' *ETC,* XXII, 2 (June 1965), 207–20.

15 Ibid., p. 148, and see pp. 140ff.

16 Ibid., p. 148.

17 Ibid., p. 147.

18 Ibid., pp. 104–5 (his capitals).

19 See Black, 'Linguistic Relativism.'
Hugo A. Bedau's review of Whorf, *Philosophy of Science,* XXIV, 3 (July 1957), 289–93.
Charles F. Hocket, in Harry Hoijer, ed., *Language and Culture* (Chicago, 1954), p. 127.

20 In Hoijer, ed., *Language and Culture,* p. 220.

21 Abraham Kaplan, in Hoijer, ed., *Language and Culture,* pp. 237–28.

22 Stephen Ullman, 'Semantic Universals,' in J.H. Greenberg, ed., *Universals of Language* (Cambridge, Mass., 1963), pp. 172–207 passim, and esp. 176–88.

23 Bedau, p. 290.

24 Hoijer, in Hoijer, ed., *Language and Culture,* p. 95.

25 G.E. von Grünbaum, in Hoijer, ed., *Language and Culture,* p. 228.

26 W.V.O. Quine, *Word and Object* (Cambridge, Mass., 1960), pp. 77–8.

27 Ibid., pp. 22, 23.
W.V.O. Quine, 'On the Reasons for Indeterminacy of Translation,' *Journal of Philosophy,* LXVIII, 6 (Mar. 1970), 178–83.

28 See *Word and Object,* p. 221, where Quine speaks of science 'limning the true and ultimate structure of reality,' and ibid., pp. 24–5, where he rejects 'a relativistic doctrine of truth' (but in connection with the latter view, see the section on 'Scepticism' below).
See also W.V.O. Quine, 'Replies to Chomsky,' in Donald Davidson and Joakko Hintikka, eds., *Words and Objections* (Dordrecht, Holland, 1969), pp. 302–4.

29 Quine, *Word and Object*, pp. 73ff.
30 See Quine, 'Indeterminacy,' and below.
31 More than one criticism of Quine's attack on analyticity and synonymy argued that our ability to translate constitutes a *prima facie* case for there being sameness of meaning relations among linguistic expressions (see the well known 'In Defense of a Dogma,' by H.P. Grice and P.F. Strawson, *The Philosophical Review*, LXV, 2 [Apr. 1956], 141–58); Quine's argument in *Word and Object* could be viewed as an attempt to show that 'successful translation' can be analyzed without reference to sameness of meaning.
    See Daniel Goldstick, 'A Practical Refutation of Empiricism,' Oxford University diss., 1968, appendix II.
32 Whorf, *Language*, p. 58 (his capitals).
33 Ibid., pp. 67–8.
34 Kaplan, in Hoijer, ed., *Language and Culture*, pp. 139–40; although at p. 207 he criticizes Whorf along lines similar to the one suggested here.
35 J.H. Greenberg, in Hoijer, ed., *Language and Culture*, pp. 17–18.
36 Quoted in Basilius, 'Neo-Humboldtian,' p.100.
37 Whorf, *Language*, pp. 212–14 (his capitals).
38 Paul Henle, et al., *Language, Thought, and Culture* (Ann Arbor, 1958), p. 7.
    Ullman, 'Universals,' pp. 198–9.
39 Whorf, *Language*, pp. 215, 234–5.
40 Cicourel, *Method and Measurement*, chap. 1, esp. pp. 17–18.
    Ernest Nagel, 'Measurement,' in A. Danto and S. Morgenbesser, eds., *Philosophy of Science* (New York, 1960), pp. 121–40, first publ. in *Erkenntnis*, II Band, Heft 5 (1932), 313–33.
    Cicourel cites (without criticizing it) this very article in his chapter on measurement.
41 See Paul F. Lazarsfeld's discussion of 'expressive and predictive indicators' in his 'Problems in Methodology,' in R.K. Merton, et al., eds., *Sociology Today* (New York, 1959), I, 39–78, esp. 49ff.
42 P.K. Feyerabend, 'Explanation, Reduction, and Empiricism,' in Herbert Feigl and Grover Maxwell, eds., *Minnesota Studies in the Philosophy of Science* (Minneapolis, 1962), III, 94; see also pp. 28–9, 38–40, 50–1, 76–82, 93–4.
43 Ibid., p. 29.
44 Israel Scheffler, *Science and Subjectivity* (Indianapolis, 1967), p. 57.
45 Mary Hesse, 'Ramifications of "Grue," ' *British Journal for the Philosophy of Science*, XX, 1 (May 1969), 13–25.
46 Thus Ernest Gellner, *Words and Things* (London, 1959), attacks appeals to ordinary language (passim).

Peter Alexander, *Sensationalism and Scientific Explanation* (London, 1963), pp. 83ff, especially chap. 3, argues that sense datum theories cannot be relied on to support objectivism.

47 This widespread view is expressed by Quine, for example, *Word and Object,* pp. 24–5.

48 Nor could the scepticism be avoided by embracing fideism and saying that it is psychologically possible for a person in such a circumstance not to fall into sceptical doubt, but to go ahead and hold his belief without believing it justified. This is a psychologically dubious view. The beliefs that a person holds, the ones he considers true, are the ones on which he acts in appropriate circumstances, and it is hard to see how he could not be psychologically well disposed (consciously or otherwise) toward those *means* by which he has arrived at and/or sustains the beliefs he has. If he does not hold (consciously or unconsciously) that they are good means of gaining true beliefs, he would be hesitant to act on the beliefs. But what is it to hold that a belief has been arrived at by (usually) good means than to hold that it is justified?

In the above arguments, as well as in the development of my thought about scepticism in general, I am indebted to discussions with Daniel Goldstick and his 'A Practical Refutation of Empiricism,' Oxford Univ. diss., 1968; see especially part I, sections 4, 6, 12. And see his 'Methodological Conservatism,' *American Philosophical Quarterly*, VIII, 2 (Apr. 1971), 186–96.

49 One critic of linguistic relativism classifies all versions of strong linguistic relativism as variations on Kant: J.W. Swanson, 'Linguistic Relativity and Translation,' *Philosophy and Phenomenological Research*, XXXII, 2 (Dec. 1961), 185–92.

50 In addition to his 'Explanation' see Feyerabend's 'An Attempt at a Realistic Interpretation of Experience,' *Proceedings of the Aristotelian Society*, n.s. LVIII (1958), 143–70.

51 Against the position argued by Feyerabend the point is made by most of his critics that it obliterates the sense-reference distinction and hence loses any way of determining when theories are rivals. See the following:
Alexander, *Sensationalism and Scientific Explanation,* pp. 83ff.
Robert Butts, 'Feyerabend and the Pragmatic Theory of Observation,' *Philosophy of Science*, XXXIII, 4 (Dec. 1966), 382–94.
Scheffler, *Science and Subjectivity*, chap. 3.

52 Quine, *Word and Object*, pp. 17, 23, 31.

53 Michael Polanyi, *Personal Knowledge* (London, 1958), pp. 59–60.
See Rudolph Carnap, 'Empiricism, Semantics, and Ontology,' in *Meaning and Necessity,* rev. ed. (Chicago, 1956), pp. 205–21.
I believe this view is also expressed by Vilfredo Pareto, *The Mind and Soci-*

ety, trans. A. Bongiorno and A. Livingston (New York, 1935), I, 13–14.

54 R.L. Goodstein, 'Language and Experience,' in Danto and Morgenbesser, eds., *Philosophy of Science* pp. 82–100; originally publ. in R.L. Goodstein, *Constructive Formalism* (Leicester, 1965), chap. 8.

CHAPTER FOUR

1 Charles H. Cooley, *Sociological Theory and Social Research* (New York, 1930), p. 297.

2 See P.K. Feyerabend, 'Explanation, Reduction, and Empiricism,' in Herbert Feigl and Grover Maxwell, eds., *Minnesota Studies in the Philosophy of Science* (Minneapolis, 1962), III, passim, esp. 36ff.
   N.R. Hanson, *Patterns of Discovery* (Cambridge, 1958), chap. 1.

3 See the passage from Whorf quoted above and a defence of this view by F.G. Lounsbury, in Harry Hoijer, ed., *Language and Culture* (Chicago, 1954), p. 137.
   See also L. von Bertalanffy, 'An Essay on the Relativity of Categories,' *Philosophy of Science,* XXII, 4 (Oct. 1955), 243–62.
   Talcott Parsons, *The Structure of Social Action* (Gencoe, 1949), p. 28.

4 Peter Achinstein, 'The Problem of Theoretical Terms,' *American Philosophical Quarterly*, II, 3 (july 1965), 193–203.

5 Grover Maxwell, 'The Ontological Status of Theoretical Entities,' in Herbert Feigl and Grover Maxwell, eds., *Minnesota Studies in the Philosophy of Science* (Minneapolis, 1962), III, 3–27, esp. p. 15.

6 Richard Rudner correctly chastizes Wilfrid Sellars for confusing these debates in a symposium, and I think it was just this confusion which allowed for Hanson and Feyerabend's praise of Sellars in their comments on his paper, praise not in fact warranted by their position on objectivism. Herbert Feigl and Grover Maxwell, eds., *Current Issues in the Philosophy of Science* (New York, 1961), pp. 57–89.

7 Michael Polanyi, *Science, Faith, and Society* (Chicago, 1946), p. 11.
   Gunnar Myrdal, *Value in Social Theory* (London, 1958), pp. 154–5, 232ff.

8 Henri Bergson, *Matter and Memory* (New York, 1959), p. 23, first publ. 1911.

9 Polanyi, *Science, Faith, and Society*, p. 11.

10 Israel Scheffler, *Science and Subjectivity* (Indianapolis, 1967), pp. 28–30.
   Also see D.M. Armstrong, *A Materialist Theory of Mind* (London, 1968), pp. 246–7, in which Armstrong presents a shortened and corrected version of his defence of direct realism, originally presented by him in *Perception and the Physical World* (London, 1961), although in the 1968 book Armstrong drops the phrase 'direct realism.'

11 See Scheffler's references to findings of experimental psychology, Scheffler, *Science, Faith, and Society*, pp. 28ff.

John Madge, *The Tools of Social Science* (London, 1953), p. 123.

Leo Postman, J.S. Bruner, and E. McGinnies, 'Personal Values as Selective Factors in Perception,' *The Journal of Abnormal and Social Psychology*, XLIII (Apr. 1948), 142–54.

12 Polanyi, *Science, Faith, and Society*, p. 11.

13 Max Weber, *The Methodology of the Social Sciences*, trans. Edward Shils and Henry Finch (New York, 1949), p. 72.

14 It is in this way that Parsons tries to strengthen what is here called the argument from selection; see *Structure of Social Action*, p. 597.

15 Scheffler, *Science, Faith, and Society*, pp. 37–8.

16 Ibid., pp. 40–2.

17 Weber, *Methodology of the Social Sciences*, p. 11.

Hanson, *Patterns of Discovery*, p. 17, n3, hints at this view.

See also Myrdal, *Value in Social Theory*, pp. 128, 228; though at p. 233 he contradicts this view.

18 For a discussion of a social-scientific theory which supposes such a view see Paul Meadows, 'The Action-System Theory of Social Behavior,' in E.W. Count and G.T. Bowles, eds., *Fact and Theory in Social Science* (Syracuse, 1964), pp. 9–23.

19 E.A. Burtt, *The Metaphysical Foundations of Modern Physical Science* (New York, 1932), pp. 317–8.

20 By adding the words 'and unknowable' Burtt here betrays a Kantian-based inclination against the representative realist position, although in other places he seems to espouse representative realism.

21 Bertrand Russell, *An Inquiry into Meaning and Truth* (London, 1965), pp. 117–18, first publ. 1940.

22 See, for example, R.M. Chisholm, *Perceiving* (Ithaca, 1957), pp. 158–60.

A.M. Quinton, 'The Problem of Perception,' *Mind*, LXIV, no. 253 (Jan. 1955), 28–51.

23 Bertrand Russell, *Human Knowledge* (New York, 1948), p. 186.

G.E. Moore, 'Some Judgements of Perception,' *Proceedings of the Aristotelian Society*, n.s. XIX (1918–19), 1–29; reprinted in R.J. Swartz, ed., *Perceiving, Sensing, and Knowing* (New York, 1965), pp. 1–28, esp. pp. 5–7.

See Armstrong, *Materialist Theory*, pp. 233ff.

24 See Bertrand Russell, *Human Knowledge*, pp. 175ff.

25 Peter Alexander, *Sensationalism and Scientific Explanation* (London, 1963), passim, especially pp. 15, 43, 57, 106–7, 138.

26 Chisholm, *Perceiving*, pp. 190–1.

A.J. Ayer, *The Problem of Knowledge* (London, 1956), pp. 123–5.

Armstrong, *Perception,* chaps. 5, 6.

J.J.C. Smart, *Philosophy and Scientific Realism* (London, 1963), pp. 22ff.

27 For a similar point on sense datum theories generally, see Wilfrid Sellars, 'Empiricism and the Philosophy of Mind,' in *Science, Perception and Reality* (London, 1963), pp. 127–96, esp. pp. 138–9, 175.

28 Polanyi, *Science, Faith, and Society,* p. 11.

29 G.N.A. Vesey, 'Seeing and Seeing As,' *Proceedings of the Aristotelian Society,* n.s. LVI (1955–6), 109–124, reprinted in Swartz, ed., *Perceiving, Sensing, and Knowing,* pp. 68–83.

Ludwig Wittgenstein, *Philosophical Investigations* (New York, 1953), sec. II.xi.

Hanson, *Patterns of Discovery,* p. 19.

30 Vesey, 'Seeing,' p. 73.

31 Hanson, *Patterns of Discovery,* p. 19.

32 Ibid., p. 4.

33 Ibid., p. 19.

34 Ibid., pp. 10, 11.

35 Ibid., pp. 8, 11.

36 Ibid., p. 22.

37 Ibid., p. 25 (italics omitted).

38 Ibid., p. 25.

39 See ibid., pp. 6, 15, 23, 25, 26.

40 It is also interesting to note in this connection that Hanson denies that all seeing is 'seeing as' (*Patterns of Discovery,* p. 19) ; while he also holds that all seeing is 'seeing that.' Yet it seems that 'seeing that' presupposes 'seeing as' – to see that A is B is (at least) to see A as B, with the addition that A *is* B. Hanson plays down the role of 'seeing as,' but in his examples of 'seeing that' he seems to give this concept the role that Vesey and others give 'seeing as.' He seems to mean by phrases like 'P saw that A was B' just 'P believed that A was B' (i.e., that P had certain expectations regarding A, leaving aside the question of whether the expectations were correct, as is usually implied by 'seeing that'). The whole muddle is, I think, a result of Hanson's both rejecting representative realism and denying that visual awareness is interpretive; he illustrates the difficulty involved in defending anti-objectivism with a theory of perception.

41 Feyerabend, 'Explanation,' p. 37.

See also Abraham Kaplan, *The Conduct of Inquiry* (San Francisco, 1964), pp. 58–59.

42 J.J.C. Smart, *Between Science and Philosophy* (New York, 1968), p. 154.

Sellars, 'Being and Being Known,' in *Science, Perception and Reality,* pp. 51–4 (although I am not entirely clear about whether Sellars's overall philosophical position is correctly counted as an objectivist one).

CHAPTER FIVE

1 Quentin Gibson, *The Logic of Social Enquiry* (London, 1960), pp. 9–10.
See also Richard Rudner, *Philosophy of Social Science* (Englewood Cliffs, 1966), p. 70.
The view that man is unique is, in fact, usually (but not always clearly) conjoined with some designation of the qualities which make him unique. E.g., Heinrich Rickert, *Science and History*, trans. George Reisman (New York, 1962) links the uniqueness view, often associated with his name, with the view to be discussed below that human acts of evaluating and purposive activity generally are the proper objects of social-scientific study (in his discussion of the distinction between what Windleband called the 'nomothetic' and 'idiographic').
See also Wilhelm Windelband, *An Introduction to Philosophy*, trans. J.H. Tufts (London, 1921), pp. 57, 98–103, and chap. 9, passim.

2 See Louis Trenchard More, 'The Pretensions of Science,' in Norman Foerster, ed., *Humanism and America* (Pt Washington, New York, 1930), pp. 3–24, where he criticizes social science for being unable to comprehend the 'whole man.'
This problem, among others, is examined by Paul Ricoeur, 'The Antinomy of Human Reality and the Problem of Philosophical Anthropology,' in N. Lawrence and D. O'Connor, eds., *Readings in Existential Phenomenology* (Englewood Cliffs, 1967), pp. 390–402, originally published in *Il Pensiero*, v (1960), 273–90, trans. Daniel O'Connor.

3 See, for example, Isaiah Berlin's *Historical Inevitability* (London, 1954).

4 Jacques Lacan, quoted in Peter Caws, 'What is Structuralism?' *Partisan Review*, xxxv, 1 (Winter 1968), 75–61.

5 Caws, 'What is Structuralism?' p. 85.

6 See Jean-Paul Sartre, 'Existentialism is a Humanism,' in *Existentialism and Human Emotions* (New York, 1957), p. 15.
Wilhelm Dilthey, *Pattern and Meaning in History,* trans. H.P. Rickman (New York, 1962), pp. 73–74, 78, 81–2. The selections translated here were originally published in 1905; Dilthey is unclear in these passages as to whether he thinks individuals may have other characteristics than being points of intersecting systems.
G.H. Mead, *The Social Psychology of G.H. Mead,* ed. Anselm Strauss (Chicago, 1959), part 3. It should be noted that neither Mead nor Dilthey is, at least at the places cited, defending anti-objectivism.

7 Max Weber, *The Theory of Social and Economic Organization,* trans. A.M. Henderson and Talcott Parsons (Glencoe, 1964), pp. 90ff.

8 See David Braybrooke, ed., *Philosophical Problems of the Social Sciences* (New York, 1965); and T.W. Wann, ed., *Behaviorism and Phenomenology* (Chicago, 1964). These anthologies are organized around the debates

between members of these two camps.

9 An example can be seen in Vilfredo Pareto's *The Mind and Society*, trans.
   A. Bongiorno and A. Livingston (New York, 1935), vol. I, where the two
   uses are mixed up in such a way as to make an important section almost unin-
   telligible. In discussing agents' aims Pareto uses 'subjective' to mean something like 'as the aims appear to the agent' and 'objective' to mean 'as the
   aims really are' (pp. 76ff). Using a Weberian sense of 'subjective,' aims just
   are what agents see as their ends, so there could be no distinction between
   aims as they are in themselves and as they appear; this distinction makes
   sense on the meaning of 'objective' opposed not to 'subjective' but to 'not-
   objective' as used in the present work.

10 Ludwig von Mises, *Theory and History* (London, 1958), p. 11.

11 F.A. Hayek, *The Counter-Revolution of Science* (Glencoe, 1955), pp. 22ff.
   Alfred Schutz, 'Concept and Theory Formation in the Social Sciences,'
   'Common Sense and Scientific Interpretation of Human Action,' in Maurice
   Natanson, ed., *Philosophy of the Social Sciences* (New York, 1963), pp.
   231–49 and 302–46 respectively; see esp. pp. 242, 305; these articles appeared
   originally in *Journal of Philosophy*, LI, 9 (Apr. 1954), 257–273 and in
   Philosophy and Phenomenological Research, XIV, 1 (Sept. 1953), 1–37
   respectively.
   Florian Znaniecki, *The Method of Sociology* (New York, 1934), see pp. 37ff.

12 R.M. MacIver, *Society* (New York, 1931), p. 530.

13 Talcott Parsons, *The Structure of Social Action* (Glencoe, 1949), p. 44.

14 von Mises, *Theory and History*, pp. 19–20.
   Weber, *Social and Economic Organization*, pp. 92–3.

15 G.E.M. Anscombe, *Intention* (Oxford, 1963).
   A.I. Melden, *Free Action* (London, 1961).
   Stuart Hampshire and H.L.A. Hart, 'Decision, Intention and Certainty,'
   Mind, LXVII, no. 265 (Jan. 1958), 1–12.
   Stuart Hampshire, *Thought and Action* (London, 1959), chap. 2.

16 Peter Winch, *The Idea of a Social Science* (London, 1958), esp. pp. 28, 30,
   32.

17 R.S. Peters, *The Concept of Motivation* (London, 1958), p. 149, and see also
   p. 7.
   See also Dorothy Emmet, *Rules, Roles, and Relations* (New York, 1966),
   pp. 15–16.

18 R.G. Collingwood, *The Idea of History* (New York, 1956), pp. 290ff, first
   publ. 1946.
   William Dray, *Laws and Explanation in History* (London, 1957), chap. 5.
   Winch, *Idea of a Social Science*, pp. 58–62.

19 Stephen Strasser, *Phenomenology and the Human Sciences* (Pittsburgh,

1963), pp. 10ff, 158ff.

Schutz, 'Concept and Theory Formation,' pp. 236–8.

Alfred Schutz, 'The Social World and the Theory of Social Action,' in David Braybrooke, ed., *Philosophical Problems of the Social Sciences* (New York, 1965), pp. 53–67, first publ. in *Social Research*, xxvii (Summer 1960), 203–21.

20 MacIver, *Society*, p. 530.

21 Gustav Bergmann and Kenneth Spence, 'Operationalism and Theory in Psychology,' *Psychological Review*, xlviii,1 (Jan. 1941), 1–14. See also by the same authors, 'The Logic of Psychophysical Measurement,' *Psychological Review*, li, 1 (Jan. 1944), 1–24.

Behaviourists themselves are not always clear on these points in their own expositions of what they are doing. See for example B.F. Skinner's 'Behaviorism at Fifty,' in Wann, ed., *Behaviourism and Phenomenology*, pp. 79–96, and the criticisms by Michael Scriven which follow.

22 See Ernest Nagel, *The Structure of Science* (New York, 1961), on the subjectivist-behaviourist controversy, pp. 477–80.

23 Hayek, *Counter-Revolution*, p. 26.

24 See John Madge, *The Tools of Social Science* (London, 1953), p. 34.

Also see the introductions and articles in Paul F. Lazarsfeld and Morris Rosenberg, eds., *The Language of Social Research* (New York, 1955).

25 Paul Diesing, 'Objectivism vs. Subjectivism in the Social Sciences, *Philosophy of Science*, xxxiii, 1 (Mar. 1966), 124–33.

26 Arthur B. Cody, 'Can a Single Action Have Many Different Descriptions?' *Inquiry*, x, 2 (Summer 1967), 164–80.

Eric D'Arcy, *Human Acts* (Oxford, 1963).

27 David Braybrooke, 'Taking Liberties with the Concept of Rules,' *Monist*, lii, 3 (July 1968), 329–58.

28 Charles Taylor, *The Explanation of Behavior* (London, 1964), chaps. 1–3.

Richard Taylor, *Action and Purpose* (Englewood Cliffs, 1966), chaps. 9, 10.

Peters, *Concept of Motivation*, see pp. 7, 149–50.

Melden, *Free Action*, chap. 9.

Winch, *Idea of a Social Science*, p. 72.

Collingwood, *Idea of History*, part 5, sec. 4.

Dray, *Laws and Explanation in History*, chap. 5.

See also Dray's 'The Historical Explanation of Actions Reconsidered,' in Sidney Hook, ed., *Philosophy and History* (New York, 1963), pp. 105–35.

29 Dray, *Laws and Explanations in History*, p. 124.

30 Nagel, *Structure of Science*, chap. 12; and see his 'Teleological Explanation and Teleological Systems,' in Herbert Feigl and May Brodbeck, eds., *Readings in the Philosophy of Science* (New York, 1953), pp. 537–58, originally

publ. in Stanley G. Ratner, ed., *Vision and Action* (Rutgers University Press, 1953).

See criticisms of Taylor's version of teleology as a general theory of explanation and as applied to human behaviour in Robert Brown's review of his book in *Philosophy*, XL, no. 154 (Oct. 1965), 344–8, and N.S. Sutherland's review in *Philosophical Quarterly*, XV, no. 61 (Oct. 1965), 379–81.

A good representation of positions in this debate is to be found in John V. Canfield, ed., *Purpose in Nature* (Englewood Cliffs, 1966).

31 See Donald Davidson's well known article, 'Actions, Reasons, and Causes,' *Journal of Philosophy*, LX, no. 23 (Nov.1963), 685–700.

See for instance, the anthologies of Sidney Hook, ed., *Philosophy and History* and William Dray, *Philosophical Analysis and History* (New York, 1966).

32 Dray, *Laws and Explanation in History*, pp. 129–31.

33 Charles Taylor himself has reservations about the possibility of objectivity in teleological explanation; however these derive not from his view of that kind of explanation, but from a version of perceptual relativism apparently held by him; see *Explanation of Behaviour*, pp. 75ff, 93.

34 As Gibson, among others, notes in *Social Enquiry*, p. 81.

35 Madge, *Tools of Social Science*, p. 127.

36 The argument might be advanced by social theorists by employing a suitable definition of 'person,' but surely this would restrict the scope of social science too much for even the most radical advocates of 'subjectivism.' Also someone using this argument would face such problems as what to do about 'persons' who believe that parts of their personalities are not known by them and that some of their beliefs about themselves may be objectively false.

37 Magel, *Structure of Science*, pp. 467–8.

Also Madge, *Tools of Social Science*, pp. 128–9.

38 Such a view is suggested at one point by Howard Becker, who usually advocates a subjectivist position, 'Problems of Inference and Proof in Participant Observation,' *American Sociological Review*, XXIII, 6 (Dec. 1958), 652–60.

39 See Morris Schwartz and Charlotte Green, 'Problems in Participant Observation,' *American Journal of Sociology*, LX, 4 (Jan. 1955), 343–53.

Diesing, 'Objectivism,' pp. 128–9.

Madge, *Tools of Social Science*, pp. 129ff.

Nagel, *Structure of Science*, p. 468.

40 Schutz writes: '... man, as Simmel has clearly seen, enters any social relationship merely with a part of his self and is, at the same time, always within and outside of such a relationship,' 'Common Sense,' p. 340.

41 Robert K. Merton, *Social Theory and Social Structure* (Glencoe, 1964), p.

130, and see pp. 424ff.

42 The dialogue was initiated by M. Rashwald's 'Value Judgments in the Social Sciences,' *British Journal for the Philosophy of Science* [hereafter cited as BJPS], VI, no. 23 (Nov. 1955), 186–208; and pursued by Adolf Grünbaum, 'Historical Determinism, Social Activism and Prediction in the Social Sciences,' BJPS, VII, no. 27 (Nov. 1956), 236–40.

Alan Gewirth, 'Can Men Change the Laws of Social Science,' *Philosophy of Science*, XXI, 3 (July 1954), 229–41.

Nagel, *Structure of Science*, pp. 468–9.

Karl Popper, *The Poverty of Historicism* (New York, 1964), pp. 15ff. Popper distinguishes (though not always clearly) between objectivist and anti-objectivist historicism. He criticizes the former, not for claiming objectivity, but for being over-ambitious about the possibility of general societal theories; he criticizes the latter along lines similar to Grünbaum et al. although it is interesting to note that at one stage Popper argued that the social sciences as well as the non-social ones could not be pursued deterministically for reasons similar to the ones he criticizes in *The Poverty of Historicism*; 'Indeterminism in Quantum Physics and Classical Physics,' BJPS, I, nos. 2, 3 (Aug., Nov. 1950), 117–33, 173–5.

43 Hayek, *Counter-Revolution*, 78.

44 It is not certain that Weber himself thought this method to be altogether indispensable; see *Social and Economic Organization*, p. 91.

45 Nagel, *Structure of Science*, pp. 484ff.

Rudner, *Social Science*, p. 72.

Theodore Abel, 'The Operation Called *Verstehen*,' *American Journal of Sociology*, LIV, 3 (Nov. 1948), 211–18.

Collingwood, *Idea of History*, pp. 213ff, 282.

Dray, *Laws and Explanation in History*, pp. 126ff.

Schutz, 'Concept Formation,' p. 240.

Strasser, *Phenomenology*, pp. 156ff, 170ff, 178.

46 Schutz, 'Concept Formation,' pp. 239–40, 242.

Schutz, 'Common Sense,' pp. 309–10, 337–8.

See Alfred Schutz, *The Phenomenology of the Social World*, trans. George Walsh and Frederick Lehnert (Northwestern University Press, 1967), pp. 220–3, first publ. 1932.

47 Schutz, 'Common Sense,' pp. 334–5, 339ff.

Schutz, *Phenomenology*, pp. 223ff.

There is also controversy over just what ideal types are; see the debate between Hempel and Schutz in Natanson, ed., *Philosophy of the Social Sciences*, pp. 210–50.

48 Ernest Gellner, 'Concepts and Society,' in *Transactions of the 5th World*

Congress of Sociology, I (1962), 153–83, esp. 170–3. The article is reprinted in Dorothy Emmet and Alasdair MacIntyre, eds., *Sociological Theory and Philosophical Analysis* (London, 1970), pp. 115–49. Gellner's main concern in this paper is to combat those functionalists who use the method of supplying the context in which a concept is used too charitably. Gellner's position seems to be that this contextual analysis can be objectively carried out, but not without difficulty.

See also S.F. Nadel, *The Foundations of Social Anthropology* (London, 1951), pp. 46ff.

49 The connection between phenomenology and symbolic interactionism is most clearly seen in the frequent references of symbolic interactionists to the work of Alfred Schutz.

Also see Edmund Husserl, *Cartesian Meditations,* trans. Dorion Cairns (The Hague, 1960), meditation no. 5.

50 See the essays in Jerome G. Manis and Bernard N. Meltzer, eds., *Symbolic Interaction* (Boston, 1967), esp. essay no. 9 by Herbert Blumer.

51 See Herbert Blumer, ibid., p. 142.

Edmund Husserl, *Ideas,* trans. W.R. Boyce Gibson (London, 1958), author's preface to the English edition and sec. 1, first publ. 1913; first English ed. in 1931.

52 See Herbert Blumer in Manis and Meltzer, eds., *Symbolic Interaction,* essay no. 9.

G.H. Mead, *Social Psychology.*

Schutz, *Phenomenology,* chap. 3.

53 Hayek, *Counter-Revolution,* pp. 22ff, 34ff.

Znaniecki, *Method of Sociology,* p. 49.

Collingwood, *Idea of History,* pp. 215, 243, 283.

See also Max Scheler, *Man's Place in Nature,* trans. Hans Meyerhoff (New York, 1961), esp. pp. 47–8. Scheler links this view with one similar to that expressed in the Lecan argument discussed above.

54 Winch, *Idea of a Social Science,* p. 88; see pp. 55, 83–9, 108, 182.

55 Weber, *Social and Economic Organization,* p. 91.

56 Rudner, *Social Science,* p. 69.

57 Gibson, *Social Enquiry,* pp. 52ff.

58 See Collingwood, *Idea of History,* part 5, sec. 4.

59 Winch, *Idea of a Social Science,* p. 55.

60 Ibid., pp. 58ff, 83ff.

61 Ibid, p. 87.

62 Charles H. Cooley, *Sociological Theory and Social Research* (New York, 1930), pp. 289ff.

Hayek, *Counter-Revolution,* p. 78.

Strasser, *Phenomenology,* p. 143.

William McEwen, *The Problem of Social-Scientific Knowledge* (Totowa, 1963), chap. 1.

Schutz, 'Common Sense,' pp. 309–10, 331–3, 338.

Aaron V. Cicourel, *Method and Measurement in Sociology* (Glencoe, 1964), Introduction and chap. 9.

63 Nagel, *Structure of Science,* pp. 499–500.

Felix Kaufmann, *Methodology of the Social Sciences* (New York, 1944), pp. 190–1.

Maurice Mandelbaum, *The Problem of Historical Knowledge* (New York, 1938), pp. 180ff.

64 See Nagel, *Structure of Science,* p. 500.

Gustav Bergmann, 'Ideology,' in May Brodbeck, ed., *Readings in the Philosophy of the Social Sciences* (New York, 1968), pp. 123–38, originally publ. in *Ethics,* LXI, 3 (Apr. 1951), 205–18.

Mandelbaum, *Historical Knowledge,* pp. 177–8.

65 Mannheim, *Ideology,* p. 5.

66 Merton, *Social Theory and Social Structure,* chap. 13.

67 Ibid., pp. 89ff.

68 Mannheim, *Ideology,* p. 95.

69 Peter L. Berger and Thomas Luckmann, *The Social Construction of Reality* (New York, 1967), p. 1.

Also see Stephen Strasser, *Phenomenology and the Human Sciences* (Pittsburgh, 1963), pp. 85–6.

70 Mannheim, *Ideology,* pp. 195–6.

71 There are many versions of this view, and to my knowledge it is nowhere stated clearly. But representative proponents are:

Jürgen Habermas, *Knowledge and Human Interest,* trans. J. Shapiro (Boston, 1971), esp. chap. 3 and appendix; the book was originally published in 1968, and a version of the appendix, in English translation, is in Emmet and MacIntryre, eds., *Sociological Theory and Philosophical Analysis,* pp. 36–54; also see his *Toward a Rational Society,* trans. J. Shapiro (Boston, 1970), chap. 6, 'Technology and Science as ''Ideology'' '; the book was first published in 1968.

Herbert Marcuse, *Negations,* trans. J. Shapiro (Boston, 1968), chap. 2, 'The Concept of Essence,' originally publ. 1965; also Marcuse's *One Dimensional Man* (Boston, 1964), chap. 6 and pp. 218–20; Marcuse's views are quite difficult to pin down here, but there can be no doubt that many advocates of the *Praxis* argument regarding objectivity lean heavily on some of his central points.

Lucien Goldmann, 'Is there a Marxist Sociology?' trans. I. Birchall, *Radical*

Philosophy, i (Jan. 1972), 16–22, originally in Goldmann, *Recherches Dialectiques* (Paris, 1969).

Gajo Petrovic, *Marx in the Mid-Twentieth Century* (New York, 1967), esp. pp. 117–18, 190–8.

A prominent work in the background of this view is Georg Lukács's *History and Class Consciousness,* trans. R. Livingstone (Cambridge, Mass., 1971), originally publ. 1922, republ. 1967; a good criticism of aspects of the view contained in this work and developed by Goldmann et al. is to be found in Lukács's own preface to the 1967 ed.

Also influential in the background of the view is Jean-Paul Sartre's *Critique de la Raison Dialectique* (Librarie Gallimard, 1960), the introduction to which has been translated into English by H. Barnes as *Search for a Method* (New York, 1963); a summary and defence of Sartre's work which bears on the *Praxis* argument is to be found in D.G. Cooper and R.D. Laing, *Reason and Violence* (London, 1964).

72 I have discussed the concept of practice in a way that relates to this point in 'Practice and Some Muddles about the Methodology of Historical Materialism,' to appear in *The Canadian Journal of Philosophy,* Dec. 1973.

73 For instance, Habermas seems to rest his case on varieties of the argument from values, discussed in chapter 1, and several of the arguments to show that facts are theory-laden in a way that makes objectivity impossible; and Petrovic explicitly bases his objections to the 'reflection theory of truth' (which supposes the 'old' objectivity) on the grounds, discussed in chapter 1, that objectivity is incompatible with free will or on the view, to be discussed in chapter 6, that a certain kind of social-scientific thinking is incompatible with social activism.

74 Thomas Kuhn, *The Structure of Scientific Revolutions,* 2nd ed., note ii, pp. 205–7.

75 Ibid., p. 206. There is a suggestion that Kuhn means this argument just to apply to 'whole theories' or to ones which sketch ontologies by positing unobserved entities, and possibly not to empirical description. But if so, then, in addition to facing the problems confronting anti-objectivism raised in chapter 2, he would seem to require the Carnap-like argument having to do with observation and interpretation discussed in chapter 3.

76 Mannheim, *Ideology,* pp. 300–1.

77 Nagel, *Structure of Science,* pp. 501–2.

78 Mannheim, *Ideology,* pp. 5, 224, 296–7.

79 Ibid., pp. 165, 189–90.

80 This may be implied in Mannheim's view that, by making our suppositions explicit, they are 'raised into the sphere of the controllable' (*Ideology,* p. 296). It is hard to see how the mechanics of this controlling could be spelled out

by Mannheim without supposing objectivism. E.g., if the suppositions are controlled by following them only when doing so would be likely to facilitate action in a given circumstance, then it is supposed, contrary to the general anti-objectivist thesis, that we can examine the circumstances independently of the suppositions.

81 Ibid., pp. 6ff; also see pp. 153ff.
The argument has been more recently advanced by R.W. Friedrichs, *A Sociology of Sociology* (New York, 1970), who extols 'the long-range value of "peaceful" paradigmatic co-existence,' p. 325.

82 P.K. Feyerabend, 'Reply to Criticism,' in Robert S. Cohen and Marx W. Wartofsky, eds., *Boston Studies in the Philosophy of Science* (Boston, 1965), II, 223–5.

83 Ibid., pp. 224–5.

84 Cicourel, *Method,* intro. and chap. 9, esp. pp. 19, 24.

85 Schutz, 'Common-Sense.'

86 Maurice Merleau-Ponty, 'The Philosopher and Sociology,' trans. H. Rabbin, in Mandelbaum, ed., *Historical Knowledge*, pp. 487–505; originally publ. 1951 and rep. in Merleau-Ponty, *Signes* (Paris, 1960). It is not clear whether Merleau-Ponty means his 'new idea of truth' to apply to social science or to philosophy or both.

87 Schutz, 'Common-Sense,' pp. 311–12.

CHAPTER SIX

1 The view receives widespread expression in the entertainment media where social scientists are often represented (not without a certain amount of justice) either in a comic way as unrealistically intellectualistic or as social-scientific analogues of Dr Strangelove. The following are collections of views that there is moral danger in pursuing social science:
Norman Foerster, ed., *Humanism and America* (Port Washington, NY, 1930), a collection of essays by Irving Babbitt and other proponents of the 'New Humanism.'
Helmut Schoeck and James Wiggins, eds., *Scientism and Values* (New York, 1960).
'The Application of Scientific Method to the Study of Human Behavior,' forum in *American Scholar,* XXI, 2 (Spring 1952), 208–25; esp. interesting in this symposium are the interchanges of B.F. Skinner and Joseph Wood Krutch.

2 W.H. Werkmeister, 'Theory Construction and the Problem of Objectivity,' in Llewellyn Gross, ed., *Symposium on Sociological Theory* (Evanston, 1959), pp. 483–508; the passage quoted is on p. 496.

3 See the collection of essays on this very topic by social scientists, 'The Social

Responsibilities of the Behavioral Scientist,' in *Journal of Social Issues,* xxi, 2 (Apr. 1965), 1–84.

Also see the criticisms by William T. Couch (then editor of *Collier's Encyclopedia*) of social scientists for being primarily responsible for what he sees as the 'weakening of American political conscience,' in 'Objectivity and Social Science,' in Schoeck and Wiggins, eds., *Scientism and Values,* pp. 22–49.

4 The problem in both its forms is discussed by Leonard Krasner, 'The Behavioral Scientist and Social Responsibility,' and Herbert O. Kelman in 'Manipulation of Human Behavior: An Ethical Dilemma for the Social Scientist,' both in 'The Social Responsibilities of the Behavioral Scientist,' pp. 9–30 and 30–46 respectively.

5 See Krutch's contribution to the *American Scholar* forum.

6 Eliseo Vivas, 'Science and the Studies of Man,' in Schoeck and Wiggins, eds., *Scientism and Values,* pp. 50–82; passage quoted on p. 51.

See also Vivas's, *The Moral Life and the Ethical Life* (Chicago, 1950), chap. 1.

Martin Heidegger, *An Introduction to Metaphysics,* trans. Ralph Mannheim (New York, 1961), pp. 39–40.

Isaiah Berlin, *Historical Inevitability* (London, 1954), pp. 73ff.

7 For an argument that determinism is not fatalistic, but is compatible with morality, see R.E. Hobart, 'Free Will as Involving Determinism and Inconceivable Without It,' in W. Dray, ed., *Free Will and Determinism* (New York, 1966), pp. 63–95; originally publ. in *Mind,* xliii, no. 169 (Jan. 1934), 1–27.

8 Alvin W. Gouldner, *The Coming Crisis of Western Sociology* (New York, 1970), see pp. 102–4, 175–6.

9 I for one am not satisfied that the empiricist and existential schools have adequately made out the case that scientific facts could never rationally justify moral value judgments.

10 See Paul Elmer Moore, 'The Humility of Common Sense,' in Foerster, ed., *Humanism and America,* pp. 52–74.

11 For popularly presented empirical criticisms of the Ardrey thesis see the articles in M.F. Ashley Montagu, ed., *Man and Aggression* (London, 1968). For a philosophical criticism of the view that social-scientific work supports moral relativism see V.A. Howard, 'Do Anthropologists Become Moral Relativists by Mistake?' *Inquiry,* xi, 2 (Summer 1968), 175–89.

SELECTED BIBLIOGRAPHY

SOME SOURCES OF ANTI-OBJECTIVIST ARGUMENTS

ALICOTTA, ANTONIO *The Idealist Reaction Against Science*, London, 1914

BASILIUS, HAROLD 'Neo-Humboldtian Ethnolinguistics,' *World*, XXII, 2 (June 1965), 207–20

BERLIN, ISAIAH *Historical Inevitability*, London, 1954

BURTT, E.A. *The Metaphysical Foundations of Modern Physical Science*, New York, 1932

BUTTERFIELD, HERBERT *The Origins of Modern Science*, New York, 1962

CICOUREL, AARON V. *Method and Measurement in Sociology*, Glencoe, 1964

COLLINGWOOD, R.G. *The Idea of History*, New York, 1956

COOLEY, CHARLES H. *Sociological Theory and Social Research*, New York, 1930

FEYERABEND, P.K. 'Explanation, Reduction, and Empiricism,' in Herbert Feigl and Grover Maxwell, eds., *Minnesota Studies in the Philosophy of Science*, Minneapolis, 1962, III, 28–97

HANSON, N.R. *Patterns of Discovery*, London, 1958

HAYEK, F.A. *The Counter-Revolution of Science*, Glencoe, 1955

KUHN, THOMAS S. *The Structure of Scientific Revolutions*, Chicago, 1962; enlarged ed., Chicago, 1970

LEACH, JAMES 'Explanation and Value Neutrality,' *British Journal for the Philosophy of Science*, XIX, 2 (Aug. 1968), 93–108

MacIVER, R.M. *Society*, New York, 1931

MANNHEIM, KARL *Ideology and Utopia*, New York, 1936

von MISES, LUDWIG *Theory and History*, London, 1958

MYRDAL, GUNNAR *Value in Social Theory*, London, 1958

– *Objectivity in Social Research*, New York, 1969

NADEL, S.F. *The Foundations of Social Anthropology*, London, 1951

PARSONS, TALCOTT *The Structure of Social Action*, Glencoe, 1949

POLANYI, MICHAEL *Personal Knowledge*, London 1958

– *Science, Faith, and Society*, Chicago, 1946

QUINE, W.V.O. *Word and Object*, Cambridge, Mass., 1960

TOULMIN, STEPHEN *Foresight and Understanding*, Bloomington, 1961

WEBER, MAX *The Methodology of the Social Sciences,* trans. Edward Shils and Henry Finch, New York, 1949
– *The Theory of Social and Economic Organization,* trans. A.M. Henderson and Talcott Parsons, Glencoe, 1964
WHORF, BENJAMIN LEE *Language, Thought, and Reality,* ed. John B. Carroll, Cambridge, Mass., 1964
WINCH, PETER *The Idea of a Social Science,* London, 1958

SOME SOURCES OF OBJECTIVIST ARGUMENTS

ALEXANDER, PETER *Sensationalism and Scientific Explanation,* London, 1963
BERGMANN, GUSTAV 'Imperfect Knowledge,' in May Brodbeck, ed., *Readings in the Philosophy of the Social Sciences,* New York, 1968, pp. 415–35, originally published in *Philosophy of Science,* Madison, 1957, pp. 115–24
BLACK, MAX 'Linguistic Relativism: the Views of Benjamin Lee Whorf,' in *Models and Metaphors,* Ithaca, 1962, pp. 244–57, originally published in *The Philosophical Review,* LXVIII, 2 (Apr. 1959), 228–38
BOHM, DAVID *Causality and Chance in Modern Physics,* New York, 1957
BRAITHWAITE, R.B. *Scientific Explanation,* New York, 1960
BUTTS, ROBERT E. 'Feyerabend and the Pragmatic Theory of Observation,' *Philosophy of Science,* XXXIII, 4 (Dec. 1966), 382–94
GIBSON, QUENTIN *The Logic of Social Enquiry,* London, 1960
HEMPEL, CARL G. *Aspects of Scientific Explanation,* New York, 1965
KAUFMANN, FELIX *Methodology of the Social Sciences,* New York, 1944
LENIN, V.I. *Materialism and Empirio-Criticism,* Moscow, 1964
MASON, STEPHEN F. *A History of the Sciences,* New York, 1962
NAGEL, ERNEST *The Structure of Science,* New York, 1961
RUDNER, RICHARD *Philosophy of Social Science,* Englewood Cliffs, 1966
SCHEFFLER, ISRAEL *Science and Subjectivity,* Indianapolis, 1967
SHAPERE, DUDLEY 'Meaning and Scientific Change,' in Robert G. Colodny, ed., *Mind and Cosmos,* Pittsburgh, 1966, pp. 41–85
SMART, J.J.C. *Philosophy and Scientific Realism,* London, 1963
WERKMEISTER, W.H. 'Theory Construction and the Problem of Objectivity,' in Llewellyn Gross, ed., *Symposium on Sociological Theory,* Evanston, 1959, pp. 483–508

SOME SOURCES OF BOTH OBJECTIVIST AND
ANTI-OBJECTIVIST ARGUMENTS

KAPLAN, ABRAHAM *The Conduct of Inquiry,* San Francisco, 1964
MADGE, JOHN *The Tools of Social Science,* London, 1953

MANDELBAUM, MAURICE *The Problem of Historical Knowledge,* New York, 1938

MERTON, ROBERT K. *Social Theory and Social Structure,* Glencoe, 1964

POPPER, KARL *The Poverty of Historicism,* New York, 1964

SCHUTZ, ALFRED *The Phenomenology of the Social World,* trans. George Walsh and Frederick Lehnert, Northwestern University Press, 1967

ZNANIECKI, FLORIAN *The Method of Sociology,* New York, 1934

SOME COLLECTIONS OF RELEVANT WORKS

BRAYBROOKE, DAVID, ed. *Philosophical Problems of the Social Sciences,* New York, 1965

BRODBECK, MAY, ed. *Readings in the Philosophy of the Social Sciences,* New York, 1968

DRAY, WILLIAM, ed. *Philosophical Analysis and History,* New York, 1966

EMMET, DOROTHY and MacINTYRE, ALASDAIR, eds. *Sociological Theory and Philosophical Analysis,* London, 1970

FEIGL, HERBERT and MAXWELL, GROVER, eds. *Minnesota Studies in the Philosophy of Science,* 3 vols., University of Minnesota Press, 1962

GROSS, LLEWELLYN, ed. *Symposium on Sociological Theory,* Evanston, Ill., 1959.

HOIJER, HARRY, ed. *Language and Culture,* Chicago, 1954

KRIMERMAN, LEONARD I., ed. *The Nature and Scope of Social Science,* New York, 1969

MORGENBESSER, SIDNEY and DANTO, ARTHUR, eds. *Philosophy of Science,* New York, 1960

NATANSON, MAURICE, ed. *Philosophy of the Social Sciences,* New York, 1963

SWARTZ, ROBERT J., ed. *Perceiving, Sensing, and Knowing,* New York, 1965

WANN, T.W., ed. *Behaviorism and Phenomenology,* University of Chicago Press, 1964

SELECTED INDEX